Social Issues
in Literature

Mental Illness in Ken Kesey's *One Flew over the Cuckoo's Nest*

Other Books in the Social Issues in Literature Series:

Social Issues
in Literature

Mental Illness in Ken Kesey's *One Flew over the Cuckoo's Nest*

Dedria Bryfonski, Book Editor

GREENHAVEN PRESS
A part of Gale, Cengage Learning

GALE
CENGAGE Learning™

Detroit • New York • San Francisco • New Haven, Conn • Waterville, Maine • London

GALE
CENGAGE Learning™

Christine Nasso, *Publisher*
Elizabeth Des Chenes, *Managing Editor*

© 2010 Greenhaven Press, a part of Gale, Cengage Learning

Gale and Greenhaven Press are registered trademarks used herein under license.

For more information, contact:
Greenhaven Press
27500 Drake Rd.
Farmington Hills, MI 48331-3535
Or you can visit our Internet site at gale.cengage.com

For product information and technology assistance, contact us at

Gale Customer Support, 1-800-877-4253
For permission to use material from this text or product, submit all requests online at www.cengage.com/permissions

Further permissions questions can be emailed to permissionrequest@cengage.com

Articles in Greenhaven Press anthologies are often edited for length to meet page requirements. In addition, original titles of these works are changed to clearly present the main thesis and to explicitly indicate the author's opinion. Every effort is made to ensure that Greenhaven Press accurately reflects the original intent of the authors. Every effort has been made to trace the owners of copyrighted material.

Cover image © Ted Strehinsky/Corbis.

LIBRARY OF CONGRESS CATALOGING-IN-PUBLICATION DATA

Mental illness in Ken Kesey's One flew over the cuckoo's nest / Dedria Bryfonski, book editor.
    p. cm. -- (Social issues in literature)
    Includes bibliographical references and index.
    ISBN 978-0-7377-5018-8 -- ISBN 978-0-7377-5019-5 (pbk.)
    1. Kesey, Ken. One flew over the cuckoo's nest. 2. Kesey, Ken--Criticism and interpretation. 3. Mentally ill in literature. 4. Psychiatric hospital patients in literature. I. Bryfonski, Dedria.
    PS3561.E667O536 2010
    813'.54--dc22

                                                                      2010008822

Printed in the United States of America
2 3 4 5 6 7 14 13 12 11 10

Contents

Chapter 1: Background on Ken Kesey

   A transitional figure between the Beat and Hippie movements, Kesey was the leader of the Merry Pranksters, a
   sixties countercultural group who advocated the use of
   psychedelic drugs and confrontations with conventional
   society. His works celebrate the mythic hero who engages
   in a transcendental quest for freedom, spontaneity, and
   individuality while battling a rigid, technocratic society.

   Kesey says that the drugs he took while working in a
   mental hospital gave him an altered perspective on the
   patients—he came to believe that the patients were more
   normal than their environment, a perspective reflected in
   One Flew over the Cuckoo's Nest. Drugs, however, did not
   create his narrative, they were simply a tool to get it
   written.

   There were two Ken Keseys—the public and the private.
   The public was the leader of a lively band of countercul-
   ture figures. The private authored two notable books—
   Sometimes a Great Notion and *One Flew over the
   Cuckoo's Nest*—and in his middle years lived a secluded
   life on an Oregon farm.

Chapter 2: *One Flew over the Cuckoo's Nest* and Mental Illness

Chapter 3: Contemporary Perspectives on Mental Illness

Introduction

Written in the early 1960s and taking place in the 1950s, *One Flew over the Cuckoo's Nest* is a transitional book between two very dissimilar decades. Set in a mental hospital and concerned with the threats to sanity posed by an inhumane society, the novel reflects the attitudes about mental illness and its treatment prevalent in the 1950s.

The 1950s were an era of prosperity, conformity, and tranquility for most Caucasian Americans. A popular former war hero, Dwight Eisenhower, was in the White House, and, despite the tensions of the Cold War, the mood of the country was optimistic. Challenges to this complacency were heard from only a few sources, most notably the Beat Generation, or beatniks, who were based on the West Coast around San Francisco. Beat writers such as Allen Ginsberg and Jack Kerouac challenged the materialism, patriotism, and conformity of the time in such works as "Howl" and *On the Road*, respectively.

Ken Kesey was a transitional figure from 1950s optimism to 1960s rebellion—a writer who picked up the legacy of the Beat writers who preceded him and who inspired the hippie movement and later writers of the 1960s. Kesey was living in California in the late 1950s while enrolled in a creative writing program at Stanford University and became attracted to and influenced by Beat writers.

Several movements came together in the 1960s to create an era of turbulence and social unrest. Proponents of the civil rights movement, antiwar movement, women's liberation, gay liberation, and sexual revolution all were part of a wave labeled the "counterculture." *One Flew over the Cuckoo's Nest*, which depicted the rugged individual struggling against a society that demands conformity, was embraced by the counterculture and became a defining work for the decade.

Kesey had attempted an earlier novel criticizing a conformist society. *Zoo*, an unpublished novel about beatniks living in San Francisco, was written in 1959 while he was a student at Stanford. His experiences as an aide in a mental hospital in Menlo Park, California, however, caused him to question the boundaries between sanity and insanity. With this as a theme and the mental hospital as a setting, he put aside *Zoo* and wrote *One Flew over the Cuckoo's Nest*, which became an instant success. In viewing the mental patients who surrounded him, Kesey questioned a society that defines sanity as conforming to the norms of that society. If that society is in fact barbaric, mechanized, and conformist, is it not more sane to reject that society? asks Kesey.

Institutions for the mentally ill had a checkered past in the United States. Up until the middle of the nineteenth century, there was little treatment available for the mentally disturbed. They were confined to asylums that were more like prisons, wandered the streets, or were confined to their homes by relatives. Not until attention was drawn to the inhumanity of these practices by reformers like Dorothea Dix in the late 1800s were state mental institutions established. In 1946 the National Mental Health Act established the National Institute of Mental Health and provided funding for research and treatment, and the number of hospitals grew. By 1955, half of all the hospital beds in the United States were occupied by those deemed mentally ill.

Several forms of treatment were available for mentally ill patients in the 1950s, and Kesey uses each of these methods in *Cuckoo's Nest* to symbolize how society attempts to control those it deems different. Directly following World War II, psychologists began experimenting with drugs to treat the mentally ill. Some of these treatments were dangerous and were eventually discontinued—the hallucinogen LSD was at one time used to treat schizophrenia, and Kesey took LSD as part of a CIA-sponsored research study while at Menlo Park. Other drugs, such as thorazine, were effective in combating depression, delusions, and anxiety. In *Cuckoo's Nest*, medications are portrayed as a way in which the hospital exerts control over the patients by drugging them into a compliant state.

A more controversial treatment, and one that has largely fallen out of favor, is the use of electroconvulsive or electroshock therapy. Introduced in the 1930s, electroshock therapy was widely used in the 1950s as a treatment for a variety of mental disorders. In *Cuckoo's Nest*, electroshock therapy is used not for therapeutic purposes, but as a form of punishment and retaliation.

The most controversial treatment used in *Cuckoo's Nest* is the lobotomy performed on McMurphy following his attack on Nurse Ratched. The use of lobotomies to control aggressive behavior in mental patients began in 1936, and for a while it was a standard treatment for patients with violent personalities. But while some patients were helped, others suffered irreversible brain damage. As word of these botched operations spread, most physicians ceased performing lobotomies. In *Cuckoo's Nest*, a lobotomy becomes the ultimate weapon of control, as the operation renders McMurphy vegetative. Thus, all of the methods used to treat mental patients at the time are, in Kesey's terms, turned into weapons against these patients.

Just as the culture of the 1950s was vastly different from the culture of the 1960s, treatment of the mentally ill changed dramatically. More effective drugs were developed to treat mental illness. Paired with psychotherapy, these drugs enabled many institutionalized people to return to society. Community-based care was emphasized, with the goal of getting patients into society as contributing members. Over a twenty-year period, the number of people in mental institutions was reduced by 70 percent.

One Flew over the Cuckoo's Nest continues to provide students with a powerful look at mental illness. In the selections in the current volume, in Chapters 1 and 2, critics discuss Kesey's use of a mental hospital and mental illness as a paradigm for a conformist society and how the characters in the story deal with their illness and treatment. Chapter 3 presents contemporary perspectives on mental illness, describing controversies surrounding treatments currently in use.

Chronology

1935

Ken Kesey is born in La Junta, Colorado, on September 17, the son of dairy farmers Geneva Smith Kesey and Frederick A. Kesey.

1939–45

The Kesey family relocates four times while Fred Kesey serves in the U.S. Navy during World War II.

1946

The Kesey family moves to Springfield, Oregon, where Fred Kesey establishes a dairy cooperative.

1953

Kesey graduates from high school where he is voted the most likely to succeed.

1956

Kesey marries his childhood sweetheart, Norma "Faye" Haxby, on May 20.

1957

Kesey graduates from the University of Oregon at Eugene. He is a champion wrestler in college and receives the Fred Lowe Scholarship as an outstanding wrestler in the Pacific Northwest in his weight class and barely misses qualifying for the Olympic team.

1957–60

Kesey writes two unpublished novels, *End of Autumn* and *Zoo*.

1958

Kesey receives the Woodrow Wilson Fellowship and enters the Stanford University creative writing program where he is also awarded the Wallace Stegner Fellowship.

1960

Kesey volunteers to take LSD as part of a CIA-sponsored research project at the Veterans Hospital in Menlo Park, California. He takes a job as an aide in the same hospital. The Keseys' first daughter, Shannon, is born.

1960–61

Kesey writes *One Flew over the Cuckoo's Nest*, at times while under the influence of peyote.

1961

The Keseys' son Zane is born.

1962

One Flew over the Cuckoo's Nest is published in February.

1963

The Keseys move to La Honda, California, and their son Jed is born. The stage play of *One Flew over the Cuckoo's Nest*, starring Kirk Douglas, opens on Broadway November 13.

1964

Sometimes a Great Notion is published. Kesey and the Merry Pranksters take a cross-country trip from California to New York in a Day-Glo-painted school bus driven by Neal Cassady.

1965

The Merry Pranksters stage a series of "Acid Tests," with LSD, rock music, and light shows. Kesey is arrested for possession of marijuana in April. He is convicted but appeals his conviction.

1966

Kesey is arrested again for marijuana possession, fakes his suicide, and flees to Mexico for eight months, where his daughter Sunshine is born. Sunshine is born out of wedlock by Merry Prankster Carolyn "Mountain Girl" Adams. Kesey returns to the United States in September and is arrested by the FBI in October.

1967

Kesey serves approximately five months in the San Mateo County Jail and the San Mateo County Sheriff's Honor Camp and is released in November.

1968

The Keseys move to a farm in Pleasant Hills, Oregon. Tom Wolfe's *The Electric Kool-Aid Acid Test*, based on the Merry Pranksters' cross-country journey, is published.

1971

The film version of *Sometimes a Great Notion* starring Paul Newman is released. Kesey coedits *The Last Supplement to the Whole Earth Catalogue* with Paul Krassner.

1973

Kesey's Garage Sale is published.

1974–75

Kesey travels in Egypt and writes about the pyramids for *Rolling Stone* magazine. He begins publishing a magazine, *Spit in the Ocean*.

1975

The movie version of *One Flew over the Cuckoo's Nest*, starring Jack Nicholson, is released.

1977

Kesey wins a settlement in his lawsuit against the producers of the film *One Flew over the Cuckoo's Nest.*

1977

"Seven Prayers by Grandma Whittier," a novel in progress, appears in *Spit in the Ocean.*

1982

Kesey travels to Alaska and begins writing *Sailor Song.*

1984

Kesey's son Jed is killed in a car accident on his way to a University of Oregon wrestling competition.

1986

Demon Box is published.

1987

Kesey teaches creative writing at the University of Oregon at Eugene.

1989

Caverns, a collaborative mystery novel written by Kesey and his creative writing class, is published.

1990

A children's book, *Little Tricker the Squirrel Meets Big Double the Bear*, is published. Kesey writes a screenplay, *The Further Inquiry*, based on the Merry Pranksters.

1991

The Sea Lion, a children's story, is published.

1992

Sailor Song is published.

1994

Kesey tours with members of the Merry Pranksters performing his musical play, *Twister: A Ritual Reality. Last Go Round: A Dime Western*, cowritten with Ken Babbs, is published.

1997

Kesey suffers a stroke.

2001

Kesey dies from complications following surgery for liver cancer on November 10.

Background on
Ken Kesey

The Life of Ken Kesey

Stephen L. Tanner and Laura M. Zaidman

Stephen L. Tanner is the Ralph A. Britsch Humanities Professor Emeritus of English at Brigham Young University. He has written several books on contemporary authors, including Ken Kesey *in Twayne's U.S. Authors series. Laura M. Zaidman was a professor of English at the University of South Carolina, Sumter. She has written and edited numerous works on contemporary fiction, with a specialization in children's and young adult literature.*

Ken Kesey, Tanner and Zaidman note, was a writer whose personal myth as the leader of the counterculture Merry Pranksters in the 1960s at times eclipsed his stature as writer of two first-rate novels, One Flew over the Cuckoo's Nest *and* Sometimes a Great Notion. *In his youth, Kesey pushed the envelope with his drug use; in his later years his interests turned to the occult, psychic phenomena, and Eastern religions. Unifying these two stages of his life is a transcendental quest to explore the possibilities of life.*

A writer who came of age on the West Coast during the late 1950s, Ken Kesey has been profoundly influenced by the Beats [writers of the so-called Beat movement] both in his life and in his work. Strictly speaking, he is not a Beat writer in his early books, although he admired Jack Kerouac and claims the influence of Kerouac, John Clellon Holmes, and William S. Burroughs on his prose style. Kesey is a pivotal figure between the Beats and the Hippies, the leader and chief chronicler of the activities of his associates, the Merry Prank-

Stephen L. Tanner and Laura M. Zaidman, "Ken Kesey," in *Concise Dictionary of American Literary Biography, vol. 6, Broadening Views, 1968–1988*, Detroit: Gale Research, 1989, pp. 110–19. Copyright © 1989 by Gale Research. Reproduced by permission of Gale, a part of Cengage Learning.

sters, a group of friends including Neal Cassady who helped Kesey originate the "acid tests" that popularized the use of the drug LSD in psychedelic mixed-media "happenings" in California in the 1960s. As the leader of the Merry Pranksters, described by one newspaperman as a "day-glo guerrilla squad for the LSD revolution in California," he turned from writing to search for new forms of expression induced by drugs—forms of expression in which there would be no separation between himself and the audience; it would be all one experience, with the senses opened wide. Tom Wolfe's *The Electric Kool-Aid Acid Test* (1968) chronicles this search and the escapades of the Merry Pranksters.

Early Success

Kesey was born on 17 September 1935 in La Junta, Colorado, to Fred and Geneva Smith Kesey. He attended public schools in Springfield, Oregon, where his father had moved to establish a dairy cooperative. He graduated from the University of Oregon, where he was involved in fraternities, drama, and athletics—as a champion wrestler he barely missed qualifying for the Olympics. He married his high school sweetheart, Faye Haxby, on 20 May 1956, and they had four children: Shannon, Zane, Jed, and Sunshine. After graduating from college, he worked for a year, toyed with the idea of being a movie actor, wrote an unpublished novel about college athletics, "End of Autumn," and then in 1958 began graduate work in creative writing at Stanford, studying with Wallace Stegner, Malcolm Cowley, Richard Scowcraft, and Frank O'Connor.

Kesey completed another unpublished novel, "Zoo," which deals with San Francisco's North Beach, before he began writing *One Flew over the Cuckoo's Nest* in the summer of 1960. About this time he was introduced to drugs, specifically LSD, as a paid volunteer for government drug experiments conducted at the Veterans Administration Hospital in Menlo Park, California. Soon afterward he took a job as aide in that hospital. Both the experience with drugs and the hospital work provided material for his novel, some of which he wrote during his night shifts, and, according to Kesey, some of it under the influence of peyote.

One Flew over the Cuckoo's Nest (1962) was a critical success from the beginning. Its popularity, particularly among college students, has grown steadily, with paperback sales soaring into the millions. . . .

The novel describes how a section of a mental hospital controlled efficiently by Miss Ratched, known as Big Nurse, is disrupted by the arrival of Randle Patrick McMurphy, an exuberant, fast-talking hustler fresh from a prison work farm. The story is told from the point of view of a large, schizophrenic Indian named Bromden, an inmate pretending to be deaf and mute as a defense against a society to which he cannot adapt. McMurphy, through his irrepressible energy and laughter, helps the patients, particularly Bromden, find the self-confidence and courage to rebel against the sterile, mechanistic, manipulative forces represented by Big Nurse. McMurphy is sacrificed in the process. Allusions and motifs from the Gospels, blended with those from comic books and popular culture, lend a mythic quality to the conflict between Good and Evil, with McMurphy as hero. More specifically, the forces of nature, spontaneity, motion, land freedom struggle against those of static, technological control—contemporary American society's "Combine."

The tightly organized plot consists of four symmetrical parts linked by consistent patterns of imagery associated with the opposition of nature and the machine. A central theme is the power of laughter as a source of vitality and sanity. Bromden acknowledges that McMurphy taught him "you have to laugh at the things that hurt you just to keep yourself in balance, just to keep the world from running you plumb crazy." When McMurphy has finally produced spontaneous and uninhibited laughter among his fellow inmates, his purpose as hero or savior is essentially complete. The kind of salvation he brings about is most clearly seen in Bromden's recovering his ability to sense with pleasure the natural world once again. Before McMurphy came, he lived in a numbing, hallucinated fog that he imagined was produced by machines in the hospital. . . .

Kesey's Next Novel

After finishing *One Flew over the Cuckoo's Nest* in June 1961, Kesey returned to the logging country of Oregon and began gathering material for *Sometimes a Great Notion* (1964). On mornings and evenings he rode in pickup trucks taking loggers to and from camps. At nights he visited bars where loggers went. After about four months of this, he returned to Stanford to write. In the summer of 1963 he moved to a mountain home in La Honda, fifteen miles from Palo Alto, which became the headquarters for the Merry Pranksters, and there he completed the novel.

In *Sometimes a Great Notion* a logging family defies a labor union, and thereby the whole community they live in, by continuing their logging operations during a strike. Within the family, Hank Stamper is in conflict with his half-brother, Lee, a bookish college student who has been living in the East. As a child, Lee witnessed his mother having sex with Hank, and this has disturbed him emotionally. Lee returns to avenge himself by seducing Hank's wife. In the end both brothers come to understand themselves better. Kesey has disclosed that in writing this novel he wanted to find out "which side of me really is: the woodsy, logger side—complete with homespun homilies and crackerbarrel corniness, a valid side of me that I like—or its opposition. The two Stamper brothers in the novel are each one of the ways I think I am."

Despite its stylistic and psychological complexity, this novel treats an essentially simple theme: the ability of the self-reliant individual to prevail over awesome antagonistic forces. . . .

Despite remarkable triumphs in language, the novel is somewhat strained and meandering, its experimental style at times difficult. Although it has sold well, it has achieved neither the enthusiastic praise nor the wide attention given to *One Flew over the Cuckoo's Nest.*

The Merry Pranksters

In the summer of 1964 Kesey and the Merry Pranksters, dressed in outrageous costumes and transported in a bus painted fantastically with day-glo paint, traveled to New York for the publication of *Sometimes a Great Notion.* They shot more than forty hours of film of themselves during this trip. This film came to be known as "The Movie" and was later used frequently at Prankster-sponsored drug and music presentations—the so-called "acid tests."

In 1965 Kesey was arrested for possession of marijuana. A year of hearings and court appearances followed, resulting in his conviction. Early in 1966 he fled to Mexico to avoid prosecution, but he returned after about six months and was arrested. Eventually he served sentences totaling about five months in the San Mateo County Jail and later at the San Mateo County Sheriff's Honor Camp. He was released in November 1967.

In 1968 he moved to a farm in Pleasant Hills, Oregon, where he has remained. At the time of his arrest he expressed the intention of giving up writing in favor of more "electrical forms." "I'd rather be a lightning rod than a seismograph," he explained. But later his interests returned to writing. When asked in 1971 if he had once believed writing to be an old-fashioned and artificial occupation, he replied, "I was counting on the millennium. Now I guess I'm tired of waiting."

Kesey's personal revolt during the 1960s with the Pranksters is most vividly documented in *Kesey's Garage Sale* (1973), a joint production of the Viking Press and Intrepid Trips, an informal association of Kesey and his friends Ken Babbs, Paul Foster, and Kenneth Barnes. . . .

The tone of the book is given as much by the "acidophilic artisticizing" of its illustrator Paul Foster as it is by the satiric texts. Words are less important, in fact, than images in *Kesey's Garage Sale*: the table of contents is lettered and drawn in comic-book style, and the subsequent pages have illustrations, photomontages, and typographic design in the tradition of the layout of the earliest Beat literary magazines like *Beatitude*, later developed more completely in the visual effects of Stewart Brand's *Whole Earth Catalog*. Kesey had edited a supplement issue of the *Catalog* in 1971 with Paul Krassner of the *Realist* magazine, and their collaborative efforts reappear in *Kesey's Garage Sale*. Here Kesey pays tribute to books and people who influenced his life: the Bible, the I Ching, Martin Buber, Malcolm X, Ernest Hemingway, [William] Faulkner, Burroughs, Timothy Leary, the Beatles, Woody Guthrie, Joan Baez, among others. *Kesey's Garage Sale* could in fact be deposited in a time capsule as a record of the chaotic influences that shaped the "revolutionary consciousness" of the 1960s. The collection also includes the screenplay *Over the Border*, in which Kesey immortalizes the heroic character of Neal Cassady, who had died in 1968. . . .

Over the Border can be read as a morality play conceived in the modern form of a psychedelic comic-book film scenario, with line drawings on every page representing the action dramatized in the text. The characters are based on "real life people" given comical names like "Sir Speed" Houlihan (Cassady) and transformed into cartoon figures by Kesey's exaggeration of personal characteristics and idiosyncratic speech patterns; yet just beneath the surface, under the high-camp fun and games, lies an unmistakably serious investigation, proceeding as if Kesey were evaluating his life with the Pranksters and his involvement with hallucinogenic drugs. When Deboree is ready to leave Mexico and turn north to face his

Ken Kesey. AP Images.

responsibilities in America, he is a changed man. As one of the characters describes him, "He amped out on too much something; I don't know whether it was psychedelics, electronics or heroics."

Kesey decided that the answer to the riddle was that Cassady's life "was the yoga of a man driven to the cliff-edge by the grassfire of an entire nation's burning material madness. Rather than be consumed by this burn he jumped, choosing to sort things out in the fast-flying but smogfree moments of a life with no retreat. In this commitment he placed himself irrevocably beyond category. Once, when asked why he wouldn't at least *try* to be cool, he said, 'Me trying to be cool would be like James Joyce trying to write like Herb Gold.'"

Kesey Gives Up Drugs

Kesey's renewed interest in writing has been accompanied by a turning away from drugs. He once believed that drugs like LSD could open wonderful, mind-expanding experiences. Though he might not have given up that belief entirely, he has lost interest in deliberate experimenting. "There are dues," he admits, and "even if it were safe and sanctioned we just don't have the right." "The biggest thing I've learned on dope," he said in 1970, "is that there are forces beyond human understanding that are influencing our lives." His hope and fascination now seem to be the mystique of the land, the cycles of nature, and farming for awareness, not money. He has been active in arousing public interest and participation in planning for Oregon's growth.

Since 1974 Kesey has edited a magazine called *Spit in the Ocean*, based in Eugene, Oregon. Portions of a novel in progress, "Seven Prayers by Grandma Whittier," appeared both in this magazine and in a collection, *Kesey* (1977). The central character of *Over the Border*, Devlin Deboree, appears here in a secondary role. The point of view is that of an eighty-six-year-old grandmother, a spry, self-reliant Christian woman whose compassion and understanding are brought to bear upon some unusual aspects of contemporary American society.

Demon Box (1986), somewhat like *Kesey's Garage Sale*, is a disorganized miscellany of previously published essays, short stories, and articles, with a few new pieces. Instead of being the "long rambling novel about cattle raising" that Kesey described in *Esquire* (March 1976), it is a rambling anthology of works about the legacy of the 1960s. Again using the thinly disguised autobiographical narrator Deboree, Kesey reflects on past experiences, still searching for the Merry Pranksters' vitality and freedom. His writing style has been compared to the free-association prose of the New Journalism. . . .

In *The Further Inquiry* (1990), a screenplay, Kesey reflects on the Merry Prankster years through a mock trial which pits prosecutor Chest against the Pranksters. . . .

Caverns (1990) is a mystery novel written by Kesey and thirteen creative-writing graduate students using the joint pseudonym O.U. Levon, an anagram for "University of Oregon novel." The story begins in 1934 when an itinerant evangelist named Loach discovers a cave. Decorated with archetypal drawings that challenge concepts about American archaeology and Western religion, this cavern later becomes the focus of Loach's quest for rediscovery. . . .

Kesey Struggles with Writer's Block

In a 1989 *Rolling Stone* interview, Kesey himself compares the novel-writing process to both jazz and surfing: "like jazz— where you're singing, where suddenly the voice is going forward and you're riding it, you're surfing on top of it. That is the art of writing. . . . It's as hard to find it as it is to teach somebody to find it." This project enabled Kesey to overcome the writer's block he faced trying to work on his novel *Sailor Song* (1992) after his son Jed's death in 1984.

Before completing *Sailor Song*, however, Kesey ventured into new territory: writing children's books. In *Little Tricker the Squirrel Meets Big Double the Bear* (1990), illustrated by well-known artist Barry Moser, good overcomes evil when a small squirrel stops a bullying bear's reign of terror, thus making the Ozark Mountains safe once again for the animals. . . .

Sailor Song finally appeared nearly three decades after Kesey's acclaimed novels of the 1960s. Ike Sallas, the protagonist, was a famous "ecoterrorist" before moving to an Alaskan fishing village. Although he tries hard to disengage himself from society, he returns to activism when he discovers the evil intent of a Hollywood film company which is there making a movie from a children's book. Rallying the townspeople against the sinister ways of Hollywood seems futile until an environmental disaster changes the landscape. . . .

Last Go Round: A Dime Western (1994), cowritten with Ken Babbs, depicts Johnathan E. Lee Spain, an old man from Tennessee, returning to the small eastern Oregon town of Pendleton to see a rodeo and recalling how he won the first Round Up in 1911 with the help of George Fletcher, a black rodeo legend, and Jackson Sundown, a Nez Percé Indian. Other well-known, colorful characters of the era include William "Buffalo Bill" Cody and wrestler Frank Gotch, who attempt to rig the rodeo competition; Parson Montanic, hell-raiser turned preacher; Prairie Rose Henderson, rodeo cowgirl; and John Muir, noted naturalist. Again, mixed reviews show that some critics admire Kesey's innovative, engaging style while others find his creative fictional techniques annoying. . . .

A Modern-Day Transcendentalist

At the center of Kesey's imaginative vision is the American cultural hero, particularly as revealed in popular art forms. Patterns in his novels suggest popular myths in folk tales, Westerns, and comic strips. He explicitly alludes to heroes such as Paul Bunyan, the Lone Ranger, and Captain Marvel. This fascination is perhaps a manifestation of Kesey's preoccupation with transcendence. His experimentation with drugs, interest in psychic phenomena, use of the I Ching, dabbling in Eastern religions, more recent focus on the Bible, a 1975 trip to Egypt in search of the occult Hidden Pyramid—all such characteristic behavior suggests a transcendental quest, an intense faith in infinite possibility for the individual person. His tendency toward mysticism, his distrust of political movements and revolution, and his attraction to nature, simplicity, self-reliance, and freedom all link his vision to that of the New England Transcendentalists. Kesey well deserves recognition for his strongly individualist works portraying the distinctly American counterculture.

Kesey Clarifies the Role Drugs Played in the Creation of *One Flew over the Cuckoo's Nest*

Robert Faggen and Ken Kesey

Robert Faggen, the Barton Evans and H. Andrea Neves Professor of Literature at Claremont McKenna College near Los Angeles, is the author or editor of numerous books, including Striving Towards Being: The Letters of Thomas Merton and Czeslaw Milosz. *Author of the counterculture classic* One Flew over the Cuckoo's Nest, *Ken Kesey was a leader of the psychedelic movement in the 1960s.*

Faggen interviewed Kesey at his Oregon farm during several visits in 1992 and 1993. In the following viewpoint, he transcribes key points from the interviews. Kesey states that the drugs he was given as part of a government experiment with psychedelic drugs helped give him an altered perspective on the patients he was working with at the Menlo Park Veterans Administration Center. He began to see that the greater insanity lay in the environment of the mental institution that housed the patients, not in the patients themselves. Kesey emphasizes, however, that while drugs may have helped him see certain things more clearly, they were not ultimately responsible for the creation of One Flew over the Cuckoo's Nest.

T his interview was conducted during several visits with Kesey at his Oregon farm in 1992 and 1993. He lives in a spacious barn that was built in the 1930s from a Sears Roebuck catalog. The steps ascending to his loft study are decorated, as are many parts of the barn, in bright Day-Glo colors. Kesey works late into the night, observed, as he points out, by a parliament of owls. . . .

Robert Faggen and Ken Kesey, "Ken Kesey: The Art of Fiction CXXVI," *The Paris Review*, vol. 36, no. 130, Spring 1994, pp. 58–94. Copyright © 1994 The Paris Review, Inc. Reprinted with permission of The Wylie Agency LLC.

The Influence of Neal Cassady

Interviewer [Faggen]:

What connection is there between Ken Kesey the magician prankster and Ken Kesey the writer?

Kesey:

The common denominator is the joker. It's the symbol of the prankster. Tarot scholars say that if it weren't for the fool, the rest of the cards would not exist. The rest of the cards exist for the benefit of the fool. The fool in tarot is this naive innocent spirit with a rucksack over his shoulder like [Jack] Kerouac, his eyes up into the sky like [William Butler] Yeats, and his dog biting his rump as he steps over the cliff. We found one once at a big military march in Santa Cruz. Thousands of soldiers marching by. All it took was one fool on the street corner pointing and laughing, and the soldiers began to be uncomfortable, self-conscious. That fool of [William] Shakespeare's, the actor Robert Armin, became so popular that finally Shakespeare wrote him out of Henry IV. In a book called *A Nest of Ninnies*, Armin wrote about the difference between a fool artificial and a fool natural. And the way Armin defines the two is important: the character Jack Oates is a true fool natural. He never stops being a fool to save himself; he never tries to do anything but anger his master, Sir William. A fool artificial is always trying to please; he's a lackey. Ronald McDonald is a fool artificial. [Beat author] Hunter Thompson is a fool natural. So was [silent film star Charlie Chaplin's famous character] the Little Tramp. Neal Cassady was a fool natural, the best one we knew.

Neal Cassady was a muse to the beats and became one to you as you started writing. When did you first encounter him?

It was 1960. He had just finished the two years he served in the pen. He showed up at my place on Perry Lane when I was at Stanford. He arrived in a Jeep with a blown transmission, and before I was able to get outside and see what was going on, Cassady had already stripped the transmission down into big pieces. He was talking a mile a minute, and there was a crowd of people around him. He never explained why he was there, then or later. He always thought of these events as though he was being dealt cards on a table by hands greater than ours. But that was one of my earliest impressions of him as I watched him running around, this frenetic, crazed character speaking in a monologue that sounded like [James Joyce's stream-of-consciousness novel] *Finnegans Wake* played fast forward. He had just started to get involved in the drug experiments at the hospital in Menlo Park, as I had. I thought, "Oh, my God, it could lead to this." I realized then that there was a choice. Cassady had gone down one road. I thought to myself, are you going to go down that road with [Beat authors William] Burroughs, [Allen] Ginsberg and Kerouac—at that time still unproven crazies—or are you going to take the safer road that leads to [New England novelist] John Updike. Cassady was a hero to all of us who followed the wild road, the hero who moved us all. . . .

Do you think the drug experimentation produced mostly casualties? Do you think Cassady was one?

I think most artists who, as the saying goes now, "push the envelope," wind up as casualties. If you think about the history of writers and artists, the best often don't end up with pleasant, comfortable lives; sometimes they go over the edge and lose it. I've been close to enough casualties to learn how to avoid that pitfall. Some critics like to argue that some of the beats had a death wish. Cassady certainly didn't have a death wish. He had a more-than-life wish, an eternity wish. He was trying to recapture, as Burroughs says, the realities he had lost. He was storming the reality studio and trying to take the projector from the controllers who had been running it. When that happens you are bound to have some casualties. . . .

A Different View of the World

How much of Neal Cassady went into the making of Randle P. McMurphy?

He's part of the myth. The Irish names—Kesey, Cassady, McMurphy—were all together in my mind as well as a sense of Irish blarney. That's part of the romantic naivete of Mc-Murphy. But McMurphy was born a long time before I met Neal Cassady. The character of McMurphy comes from Sunday matinees, from American westerns. He's Shane [protagonist in a film of the same name] that rides into town, shoots the bad guys, and gets killed in the course of the movie. McMurphy is a particular American cowboy hero, almost two-dimensional. He gains dimension from being viewed through the lens of Chief Bromden's Indian consciousness.

You were working at the Veterans Administration Medical Center in Menlo Park participating in experiments with psychedelic drugs. How much did those drugs affect you or help you to write Cuckoo's Nest?

I was taking mescaline and LSD. It gave me a different perspective on the people in the mental hospital, a sense that maybe they were not so crazy or as bad as the sterile environment they were living in. But psychedelics are only keys to worlds that are already there. The images are not there in the white crystals in the gelatin capsule. Drugs don't create characters or stories any more than pencils do. They are merely instruments that help get them on the page.

Do you use LSD or other drugs when you sit down to write?

It's impossible for me to write on LSD—there are more important things to think about. Hunter Thompson can do it, but I can't. It's like diving down to look at coral reefs. You can't write about what you've seen until you're back up in the boat. Almost every writer I know drinks to ease the burden of being out on the cliffs, so to speak. But writing under the influence of drugs is a little like a plumber trying to fix the pipes without being able to work the wrench.

I did write the first several pages of *Cuckoo's Nest* on peyote, and I changed very little of it. It had little effect on the plot, but the mood and particularly the voice in those first few pages remained throughout the book. There were also some sections of *Sometimes a Great Notion* written when I was taking mushrooms. Again, the effect is more on mood and voice than on vision. But for the most part, I don't write under the influence of LSD or other drugs.

Do you take notes when you use LSD or other hallucinogens?

Yes, sometimes I use a little tape recorder for notes. There's often a big difference between what you think you wrote under the influence and what you actually recorded. One time a friend of mine and I were taking LSD and thought we had written "The History and Future of the Universe." What we actually wrote down was something on the order of "If you pick your nose long enough the world will unravel." But often when I am taking LSD, there is an accessing of a universal pool of images, forms that I often find, for example, in Indian art. By the time I started taking peyote and LSD, I had already done a great deal of reading about mysticism—the Bhagavad-gita and Zen and Christian mystical texts. They helped me to interpret what I was seeing, to give it meaning. You don't just take the stuff and expect understanding. It's also important not to be in a hellish place with LSD or it can be a hellish experience. You need to be in a secure setting.

Do any of the visions you have using LSD get translated into your writing?

I'm fond of computer analogies. There are visions written on those programs that are hard to access or convert to the writing programs. I like to take it mostly for the spiritual experience.

Do you recommend LSD as a tool for writing?

No.

Class and Style

To go back to Cuckoo's Nest, *it seems that Chief Bromden's perspective is crucial. What was the origin of his character?*

Dr. Madison Presnell, the medical director of International Federation for Internal Freedom, administers LSD-25 to volunteers. The organization was founded c. 1962 by Timothy Leary and those he was doing research with. Kesey recalls working at the Veterans Administration Medical Center in Menlo Park, participating in experiments with psychedelic drugs such as mescaline and LSD. John Loengard/Time & Life Pictures/Getty Images.

Some have described Bromden as schizophrenic. But his is a philosophical craziness, not a clinical illness. I knew Indians who would eat mushrooms and sit and stare at the beach until the beach stared back at them. They're not unlike [French symbolist poet Charles] Baudelaire twisting himself so that he could look at flowers in a different way. They're still flowers, and he knows they're flowers but he also sees them as eyes, looking back at him. That's what Chief's craziness is all about. The idea is to regain control of reality so it's no longer presented by public relations people or funneled through a Coca-Cola bottle. The reaction against control is often violent and destructive and lashes out in all directions, even against things that are beneficial. If a man doesn't have a little madness, he never breaks the control-lock that gets placed on reality. It's facing the vast ocean alone, without the safety of land or boat.

My father used to take me to the Pendleton roundup in northern Oregon. He would leave me there for a couple of days. I spent time hanging around the Indians living in the area. I used to take the bus back down through the Columbia River Gorge where they were putting in the Dalles Dam to provide electricity to that part of Oregon so the fields could be irrigated. But it was also going to flood the Celilo Falls, an ancient Indian fishing ground along the Columbia. The government was using scaffolding to build the dam. When I first came to Oregon, I'd see Indians out on the scaffolds with long tridents stabbing salmon trying to get up the falls. The government had bought out their village, moved them across the road where they built new shacks for them. One time, as we got closer to this dam project, we were pulled over by the cops. We were in a big line of traffic. The bus driver got out and walked up to see what was happening. He came back and told us, "One of them crazy drunk Indians took a knife between his teeth and ran out into the highway and into the grill of an oncoming diesel truck, which was bringing conduit and piping to the dam project." I thought, "Boy that's far out."

Finally, he couldn't take it anymore. He just had to grab his knife, go out into a freeway and run into a truck. It was really the beginning of *Cuckoo's Nest*—the notion of what you have to pay for a lifestyle. It started an appreciation in me for the Indian sense of justice and drama. I mean, it's dumb and nasty, but that's class, and the fact that he had the knife between his teeth, that's style. So this Indian consciousness has been very important in all of the stuff that I write. It's not just in *Cuckoo's Nest*. The character Indian Jenny in *Sometimes a Great Notion* is very close to the character of Alice in *Sailor Song*. It is the dispossessed Indian spirit that's trying to reconnect with the white male spirit.

In describing the Native American who hurled himself at the truck, you said he had both class and style. How do you distinguish between class and style?

A woman who was a circus acrobat did one act for thirty years. She climbed atop of a 180-foot aluminum pole and stood on her head as her brother balanced her. One day she fell and died, and I remember reading about it in the paper. She fell, the pole fell, because it got too far over, and her brother couldn't keep up with it; he probably stepped on a peanut. She began to fall but she held her pose the whole way down and didn't scream. And of course she must have thought about it thousands of times, "What am I gonna do if it ever gets to the point where I know I can't stop it, it's going to go all the way over and I'm going to die. Can I hold my pose and not scream?" She did, and that's class. Paul Krassner, who was there, told me, "Yeah, but the fact that when she hit, she did the splits, that's style." So class is more important than style but they're connected. . . .

Evil Is Not Exercising Free Will

What do you see as evil in the world and how do you depict it?

In my novels and stories, evil is always the thing that seems to control. In *Cuckoo's Nest*, it's the combine. In *Some-*

times a Great Notion, it's the symbol of the river, eating away, leveling, trying to make that town the same. In *Demon Box*, the villain is entropy. That natural running-down of energy is the fear that the refrigerator is going to be empty, that we're not going to have enough of something; that fear makes you vulnerable to every kind of scam artist trying to sell a solution.

But the real villain is not entropy. It's the notion that entropy is the only choice. And there are a lot of other choices that we can find in religion, philosophy or art.

In Cuckoo's Nest, *Big Nurse is often regarded as the embodiment of evil. Do you think that is an accurate representation of her?*

Recently, I was over in Newport, at the opening of the Oregon Coast Aquarium, which has been seven years in the making. I was performing *The Sea Lion* in the Newport Performing Arts Center. Afterwards a white-haired old woman approached me and said, "Hey, you remember me?" I looked her over, and I knew I remembered her, but had no idea who she was. She said, "Lois." It still didn't click. She said, "Lois Learned, Big Nurse," and I thought, "Oh my God." She was a volunteer at Newport, long since retired from the nursing business. This was the nurse on the ward I worked on at the Menlo Park hospital. I didn't know what to think, and she didn't either, but I was glad she came up to me. I felt there was a lesson in it, the same one I had tried to teach Hollywood. She's not the villain. She might be the minion of the villain, but she's really just a big old tough ex-Army nurse who is trying to do the best she can, according to the rules that she has been given. She worked for the villain and believed in the villain, but she ain't the villain.

Do you believe that individuals have to be held accountable for evil, even if they are not the ultimate source?

I may, as they say in jail, hang the jacket on them, but I'm not the judge. I can expose something, but as you get older and hopefully wiser, you find that blame and punishment beget only more blame and punishment. I'm probably, from another person's point of view, the Big Nurse in somebody else's story. The thing that changes as you get older is your belief that certain people are bad forever or good forever. We're not. It wouldn't make any sense to write if we were. With blame, you either resist it or you pick up rocks and throw them at who's to blame. [Writer and critic] Wendell Berry talks about that when he says we all have the capacity to do evil but we have to learn to forebear it. What keeps us from being monsters are [American transcendentalist writers Ralph Waldo] Emerson and [Henry David] Thoreau and the Beatles and Bob Dylan—great artists who teach us to love and hold off on the hurt. The hurt is inside of us, and of course we can always randomly hurt something, but a great artist will teach you to love a thing and not want to possess it or alter it—just to love it. You finally have to love Big Nurse. It's the symbol behind her, the combine, that makes her do what she does. You've got to fight that, but finally you have to love them all—the poor, broken human beings, even the worst of them.

The Terror of Emptiness

What is the "real terror" in America?

When people ask me about LSD, I always make a point of telling them you can have the shit scared out of you with LSD because it exposes something, something hollow. Let's say you have been getting on your knees and bowing and worshipping; suddenly, you take LSD, and you look, and there's just a hole, there's nothing there. The Catholic church fills this hole with candles and flowers and litanies and opulence. The Protestant church fills it with hand-wringing and pumped-up squeezing emotions because they can't afford the flowers and the candles. The Jews fill this hole with weeping and browbeating and beseeching of the sky: "How long, how long are you gonna treat us like this?" The Muslims fill it with rigidity and guns and a militant ethos. But all of us know that's not what is supposed to be in that hole. After I had been at Stanford two years, I was into LSD. I began to see that the books I thought were the true accounting books—my grades, how I'd done in other schools, how I'd performed at jobs, whether I had paid off my car or not—were not at all the true books. There were other books that were being kept, real books. In those real books is the real accounting of your life. And the mind says, "Oh, this is titillating." So you want to take some more LSD and see what else is there. And soon I had the experience that everyone who's ever dabbled in psychedelics has. A big hand grabs you by the back of the neck, and you hear a voice saying, "So you want to see the books. Okay, here are the books." And it pushes your face right down into all of your cruelties and all of your meanness, all the times that you have been insensitive, intolerant, fascist, sexist. It's all there, and you read it. That's what you're really stuck with. You can't take your nose up off the books. You hate them. You hate who you are. You hate the fact that somebody has been keeping track, just as you feared. You hate it, but you can't move your arms for eight hours. Before you take any acid again you start trying to juggle the books. You start trying to be a little better person. Then you get the surprise. The next thing that happens is that you're leaning over looking at the books, and you feel the lack of the hand at the back of your neck. The thing that was forcing you to look at the books is no longer there. There's only a big hollow, the great American wild hollow, that is scarier than hell, scarier than purgatory or Satan. It's the fact that there isn't any hell or there isn't any purgatory, there isn't any Satan. And all you've got is [existentialist French philosopher and playwright Jean-Paul] Sartre sitting there with his momma—harsh, bleak, worse than guilt. And if you've got courage, you go ahead and examine that hollow. That's the wilderness that I've always wanted to explore, and it's connected to the idea of freedom, but it's a terrifying freedom. I'm working on a book called "The Seven Prayers of Grandma Whittier." The idea is to take someone who is a very strong, very devout Christian and put her into a situation in which she loses her faith and show how she wrestles and comes back from this hollow. And so my grandma, who's a hundred yeas old this year, and I are in some way linked in an excursion into her dark hole of Alzheimer's. You know she must be something even though she can't remember the Lord's Prayer or read the *Bible* anymore. She's alive, but that's it. You can go into that hollow and still come out of it and have a positive life.

And that hollow is, for you, the new wilderness?

That's the new wilderness. It's the same old wilderness, just no longer up on that hill or around that bend, or in the gully. It's the fact that there is no more hill or gully, that the hollow is there and you've got to explore the hollow with faith. If you don't have faith that there is something down there, pretty soon when you're in the hollow, you begin to get scared and start shaking. That's when you stop taking acid and start taking coke and drinking booze and start trying to fill the hollow with depressants and Valium. Real warriors like William Burroughs or [poets] Leonard Cohen or Wallace Stevens examine the hollow as well as anybody; they get in there, look far into the dark and yet come out with poetry.

Have you ever felt that you were going too far into void, getting too twisted to come out?

Many times I feel I have been way out, but I always come back. I have my family, my wife, Faye, the farm, chickens and cows. The earthly world calls out to you in clear voices that you must come back. Those earthly voices are far better than anything I've heard crying in the night.

Kesey Was the Seminal Author of the Psychedelic Era

Christopher Lehmann-Haupt

Christopher Lehmann-Haupt is an American journalist, critic, and novelist who worked for The New York Times *as a book reviewer and obituary writer until his retirement in 2006. He continues to write for the* Times *as well as to teach writing at Marymount College and the College of Mount Saint Vincent.*

In the following viewpoint published as Ken Kesey's obituary in The New York Times, *Lehmann-Haupt distinguishes between the two aspects of the writer—the public persona and the private man. The public Kesey was one of the flamboyant figures of the 1960s as the leader of the Merry Pranksters; the private Kesey created* One Flew over the Cuckoo's Nest, *an artistic achievement as one of the defining books of the mid-twentieth century. Although Kesey continued to write throughout his life, he was unable to recapture the magic of his first published novel.*

Ken Kesey, the Pied Piper of the psychedelic era, who was best known as the author of the novel *One Flew Over the Cuckoo's Nest*, died yesterday in a hospital in Eugene, Ore., said his wife, Faye. He was 66 and lived in Pleasant Hill, Ore.

The Public Ken Kesey

Mr. Kesey was also well known as the hero of Tom Wolfe's nonfiction book about psychedelic drugs, *The Electric Kool-Aid Acid Test* (1968). An early flowering of Mr. Wolfe's innovative new-journalism style, the book somewhat mockingly compared Mr. Kesey to the leaders of the world's great religions, dispensing to his followers not spiritual balm but quantities of lysergic acid diethylamide, or LSD, to enhance their search for the universe within themselves.

The book's narrative focused on a series of quests undertaken by Mr. Kesey in the 1960's. First, there was the transcontinental trip with a band of friends he named the Merry Pranksters, aboard a 1939 International Harvester bus called Further (it was painted as "Furthur" on the bus). It was wired for sound and painted riotously in Day-Glo colors. Neal Cassady, the Dean Moriarty of Jack Kerouac's *On the Road,* was recruited to drive. The journey, which took the Pranksters from La Honda, Calif., to New York City and back, was timed to coincide with the 1964 New York World's Fair. Its purposes were to film and tape an extended movie, to experience roadway America while high on acid and to practice "tootling the multitudes," as Mr. Wolfe put it, referring to the way a Prankster would stand with a flute on the bus's roof and play sounds to imitate people's various reactions to the bus.

"The sense of communication in this country has damn near atrophied," Mr. Kesey told an interviewer from *Publishers Weekly* after the bus arrived in New York City. "But we found as we went along it got easier to make contact with people. If people could just understand it is possible to be different without being a threat."

Then, back in California, there were the so-called Acid Tests that Mr. Kesey organized—parties with music and strobe lights where he and his friends served LSD-laced Kool-Aid to members of the public and challenged them to avoid "freaking out," as Mr. Wolfe put it. They were interrupted by Mr. Kesey's flight to Mexico in January 1966 to avoid going on trial on charges of possession of marijuana. Finally, after he returned to the United States in October and was arrested again and waiting to stand trial, there was the final Acid Test, the graduation ceremony ostensibly designed to persuade people to go beyond drugs and achieve a mind-altered state without LSD.

This was the public Ken Kesey, the magnetic leader who built a bridge from beatniks on the road to hippies in Haight-Ashbury; who brewed the cultural mix that fermented everything from psychedelic art to acid-rock groups like the Grateful Dead and Jefferson Airplane to the Trips Festival dance concerts in the Fillmore auditorium in San Francisco; and who, in the process of his pilgrimage, blew an entire generation's mind.

The Private Ken Kesey

Yet Mr. Wolfe also narrated the adventures of a more private Ken Kesey, one who in addition to his quests took the inner trips that gave him his best fiction. It is true that by 1959, when he had his first experience with drugs, he had already produced a novel, *End of Autumn*, about college athletics, although it would never be published. But after he volunteered at a hospital to be a paid subject of experiments with little-known psychomimetic drugs—drugs that bring on temporary states resembling psychosis—his imagination underwent a startling change.

To earn extra money and to work on a novel called *Zoo*, about the beatniks of the North Beach community in San Francisco, Mr. Kesey also took a job as a night attendant on the psychiatric ward of the hospital. Watching the patients there convinced him that they were locked into a system that was the very opposite of therapeutic, and it provided the raw material for *One Flew Over the Cuckoo's Nest*. One night on the ward, high on peyote, he suddenly envisioned what Mr. Wolfe described as "a full-blown Indian—Chief Broom—the solution, the whole mothering key, to the novel."

As Mr. Kesey explained, his discovery of Chief Broom, despite not knowing anything about American Indians, gave him a character from whose point of view he could depict a schizophrenic state of mind and at the same time describe objectively the battle of wills between two other key characters, the new inmate Randle Patrick McMurphy, who undertook to fight the system, and the tyrannical Big Nurse, Miss Ratched, who ended up lobotomizing McMurphy. Chief Broom's unstable mental state and Mr. Kesey's imagining of it, presumably with the help of hallucinogenic drugs, also allowed the author to elevate the hospital into what he saw as a metaphor of repressive America, which Chief Broom called the Combine.

Mr. Kesey would "write like mad under the drugs," as Mr. Wolfe put it, and then cut what he saw was "junk" after he came down.

Cuckoo's Nest was published by Viking Press in early 1962 to enthusiastic reviews. *Time* magazine call it "a roar of protest against middlebrow society's Rules and the invisible Rulers who enforce them." . . .

Although Mr. Kesey wrote several more books during his life, *Cuckoo's Nest* remained the high point of his career.

Sometimes a Great Notion followed in 1964. It was a longer and more ambitious novel about an Oregon logging family and, in the strife between two brothers, the conflict between West Coast individualism and East Coast intellectualism. Written under the influence of both drugs and Mr. Kesey's exposure to modern literature—"an *Absalom, Absalom!* [book by William Faulkner] set in Oregon," one critic called it—the novel received mixed reviews, some impressed by its energy and others annoyed by its wordiness. In 1971, a film version appeared, directed by Paul Newman and starring Mr. Newman, Henry Fonda and Lee Remick. It left so little an impression that when it was released for television, its title was changed to "Never Give an Inch."

Initially Mr. Kesey acted undaunted by the negative reaction to the novel's appearance, which was timed for the arrival of the Pranksters in New York. He told his bus mates that writing was an old-fashioned and artificial form, and that they were transcending it with their experiments in metaconscious-

The designs on this 1960s Volkswagen van are typical of the psychedelic art associated with hippies and with drug use in that decade. Image copyright © Ivan Cholakov/Gostock-dot-net, 2010. Used under license from Shutterstock.com.

ness. A decade later, however, he told an interviewer, "The thing about writers is that they never seem to get any better than their first work," and, "This bothers me a lot." He added: "You look back and their last work is no improvement on their first. I feel I have an obligation to improve, and I worry about that."

Later Works Fall Short

Yet he never did surpass his first two books. During the remainder of his life, he published two more novels, *Sailor Song* (1992), about civilization contending with nature in Alaska, and *Last Go Round: A Dime Western* (1994), an account of a famous Oregon rodeo written in the form of pulp fiction, with research done by his friend and fellow Prankster, Mr. [Ken] Babbs. He also published three nonfiction works, *Kesey's Garage Sale* (1973), a miscellany of essays by himself and others; *Demon Box* (1986), a mix of essays and stories; and *The Further Inquiry* (1990), his own history of the Prankster bus

47

trip, as well as two children's books, *Little Tricker the Squirrel Meets Big Double the Bear* (1990), which he often performed to music, and *The Sea Lion: A Story of the Sea Cliff People* (1991).

Ken Elton Kesey was born on Sept. 17, 1935, in La Junta, Colo., the older of two sons born to the dairy farmers Fred A. and Geneva Smith Kesey. Early in his life, the family migrated to Springfield, Ore., where he underwent a rugged upbringing. Although following the move his father founded a prosperous marketing cooperative for dairy farmers, the Eugene Farmers Cooperative, and established the family in a comfortable suburban setting, Mr. Kesey and his brother were taught early to hunt, fish and swim, as well as to box, wrestle and shoot the rapids of the local rivers on inner-tube rafts.

These all-American he-man lessons took, at least up to a point. Mr. Kesey developed great physical power; Mr. Wolfe writes that "he had an Oregon country drawl and too many muscles and calluses on his hands." He became a star football player and wrestler in high school and was voted "most likely to succeed" in the graduating class of 1953. At the University of Oregon, where he devoted himself to sports and fraternities, he acted in college plays and he won the Fred Lowe Scholarship, awarded to the outstanding wrestler in the Northwest. In May 1956, he married Norma Faye Haxby, his high school sweetheart. He even considered trying to become a movie star, moving to Los Angeles after graduation and playing bit parts in several films.

But his imagination exerted a counterattraction. After graduating from Oregon in 1957 and winning scholarships to Stanford University's graduate writing program, he moved to Perry Lane, the bohemian section of Palo Alto.

There he met Vic Lovell, a graduate student in psychology who told him about the drug experiments at the Veterans Administration Hospital in Menlo Park that were paying $75 a session to volunteer subjects. His journey to the interior began.

After the bus trip, the Acid Tests, and a six-month sentence on a work farm in 1967 for drug possession, he moved back to his father's farm in Pleasant Hill.

Shunning a second Prankster bus trip in 1969, its destination this time the Woodstock rock festival in the New York countryside, he settled down with his wife to raise their children—Shannon, Zane, Jed and Sunshine—work the farm, involve himself in community activities and write. In later years he insisted that he had always been a family man with strong ties to the community.

Over the next three decades, he raised cattle and sheep, and grew blueberries. He joined school boards; helped out several local businesses; ran a Web site, Intrepid Trips; edited a magazine, *Spit in the Ocean*, which he founded in 1974; and worked on completing the films and tapes of the bus trip. He coached wrestling at several local schools and taught a graduate writing seminar at the University of Oregon, in which he collaborated with 13 students on *Caverns*, a mystery published in 1990 under the pen name O.U. Levon. He practiced his lifelong hobby of magic, developing a trick in which he made a rabbit disappear. He occasionally visited the original Prankster bus, which he kept hidden in the woods on his farm.

As for drugs, Mr. Kesey's relationship with them was revealed in an interview last April [2001] in *The Times Union* of Albany [New York]. Two weeks earlier, he told the interviewer, Doug Blackburn, he and a few close friends had gone on their annual Easter Sunday hike up Mount Pisgah, near his home. For the first time in more than three decades, he had decided to skip LSD for the event. Having recently taken medication for both diabetes and hepatitis C, he said that an additional substance was unnecessary.

"I felt like I was high enough just walking up the hill with nothing but adrenaline," he said. "Besides, I figured I ought to try making the hike at least once without psychedelics. The past few years that's been the about the only time I've taken acid, and even then not much. Just enough to make the leaves dapple."

Defying Terror Was a Kesey Hallmark

Douglas Brinkley

Douglas Brinkley is a professor of history at Rice University in Houston, Texas. He is the author of numerous works, including the American Heritage History of the United States, *and is the authorized biographer of the Beat generation author Jack Kerouac.*

In his obituary of Ken Kesey, Brinkley writes that Kesey's response to the terrorist attacks on September 11, 2001, was consistent with his lifelong principles. In his early fiction, Kesey celebrated the triumph of rugged individualism against an oppressive society. He also warned of the threat of global disaster in his later works, Sailor Song *and his play* Twister. *Although Kesey was appalled at the attacks, he was against retaliation by starting another war, an opinion that was highly unpopular during the patriotic fervor that characterized the early days after 9/11. Throughout his life, Kesey distrusted big government and authority and championed the individual.*

The Willamette Valley was still blanketed in a misty predawn darkness when the horrendous news hit an Oregon dairy farmer named Ken Kesey, author of such enduring fictional classics as *One Flew Over the Cuckoo's Nest* and *Sometimes a Great Notion*: Suicidal terrorists had attacked the World Trade Center and the Pentagon, killing more than 4,300 people. "Everything was so clear that day, so unencumbered by theories and opinions, by thought, even," the 66-year-old novelist e-mailed friends 10 days after the tragedy. "It just was. All just newborn images, ripped fresh from that monstrous

Douglas Brinkley, "A Final Word from the Last Merry Prankster," *Los Angeles Times Book Review*, November 18, 2001, p. 7. Reproduced by permission.

pair of thighs thrust smoking into the morning sunshine. All just amateur cameras allowing us to witness the developing drama in sweeping handheld seizures. All just muffled mikes recording murmured gasps."

Kesey's Vision of Terror

On that fateful day, Kesey—who died of liver cancer on Nov. 10 [2001] in Eugene, Ore.—was gripped by sadness but not by The Fear. For decades in his robust fiction, intrepid bus trips and renegade proclamations, he had warned of future disasters and the need to overcome them with bedrock courage and stoical perseverance, just like the 300,000 sturdy pioneers who struggled along the Oregon Trail in the 1840s. "Throughout the work of James Fenimore Cooper there is what I call the American Terror," Kesey told *The Paris Review* in 1994. "It's very important to our literature, and it's important to who we are: the terror of the Hurons out there, the terror of the bear, the avalanche, the tornado—whatever may be over the next horizon."

Readers first encountered Kesey's vision of terror in his 1962 classic *One Flew Over the Cuckoo's Nest*, in which a modern psychiatric ward became a chilling metaphor for oppressive American society. The roguish, Randle Patrick McMurphy, is rewarded with a frontal lobotomy by the book's end. Defiance in the face of terror and unjust circumstances became a Kesey hallmark. His second novel, *Sometimes a Great Notion*, is about a stubborn Oregon logging family, the Stampers. Their maxim—which appears as a central theme throughout the sprawling narrative—is: "Never give a inch!" The entire book is a gritty Pacific Northwest adaptation of Ralph Waldo Emerson's seminal essay "Self-Reliance." Kesey understood that rugged individualism is the prize attribute in a society dominated by nuclear weapons, Orwellian Groupthink and Public Opinion Polls. Following the success of *Sometimes a Great Notion*, Kesey exploded on the consciousness of our culture when he threw an LSD party in San Francisco and saw half of America show up. Overnight he became an outlaw celebrity, "the last wagon master," as [author] Larry McMurtry called him, for painting a 1939 International Harvester bus named "Furthur" in Day-Glo colors and traveling from California to New York with his happy cohorts, known as the Merry Pranksters. Their goal was to unsettle America with their goofy LSD-inspired antics.

Kesey Was a Moralist

Lost in this semi-cartoonish portrayal—popularized by Tom Wolfe in his best-selling *Electric Kool-Aid Acid Test*—was the most important side of the real Kesey: the public moralist. Convinced that the military-industrial complex was menacing the survival of democracy, Kesey used his psychedelic bus to jar the mores of conventionality that blindly believed [U.S. president] Lyndon Johnson's claim that we were winning the Vietnam War or DuPont Chemical Co.'s assurances that it wasn't polluting the Great Lakes. "What we hoped," Kesey later noted with apocalyptic brooding, "was that we could stop the coming end of the world."

Although Kesey abandoned novel writing for 28 years following *Sometimes a Great Notion*, he returned to the genre with the publication in 1992 of *Sailor Song*, a futuristic saga of human survival that takes place in a flyspeck Alaskan fishing village called Kuinak. The lead character, Ike Sallas, is an Earth First!-type eco-radical straight out of the pages of an Edward Abbey novel. But it's really too late. Global warming (or The Effect) is slowly melting the polar caps and when Sallas is marooned in an inflatable motorboat during a storm's ferocious peak, a direct result of The Effect, he lounges back in the boat's bottom and lets it run into the strong wind. "Might as well try to get comfortable," Sallas says. "You never know how long the End of the World is liable to take."

Kesey's exploration of global disaster was explored even further in his play *Twister: A Ritual Reality in Four Quarters*, premiered in 1993 following a Grateful Dead concert in Eugene. The play—in which Kesey played the main character—is structured around the characters from Frank Baum's *The Wizard of Oz*, all of whom are confronted with third millennium crises: The Hungry Wind, The Lonely Virus and The Restless Earth. Baum's memorable characters are hammered with inconveniences such as tornadoes, plagues and earthquakes—all of which Kesey insisted were increasing in both frequency and velocity.

Kesey's Reaction to 9-11

Given his penchant for contemplating the unexpected, Kesey's e-mail reaction to the absurd terrorist attacks of September is worth considering. His first inclination was to conjure up a distant historical analogy. "Well, I can remember Pearl Harbor," Kesey wrote. "I was only six but that memory is forever smashed into my memory like a bomb into a metal deck. Hate for the Japanese nation still smolders occasionally from the hole. This 9-11 nastiness is different. There is no nation to blame. There are no diving Zeros [Japanese fighter planes], no island grabbing armies, no seas filled with battleships and carriers. Just a couple dozen batty guys with box knives and absolute purpose. Dead now. Vaporized."

But when it came to retaliating against the Taliban for the heinous crimes, Kesey turned pacifist. He had been staunchly against the Persian Gulf War and was in full dissent mode when it came to another U.S. war in the Middle East. His literary explorations in human nature had convinced him that an eye for an eye philosophy was bankrupt. "Of course we want their leaders," Kesey wrote, "but I'll be damned if I can see how we're gonna get those leaders by deploying our aircraft carriers and launching our mighty air power so we can begin bombing the crippled orphans in the rocky, leafless, already bombed-out rubble of Afghanistan." And while 90% of the American people—including me—thought President George W. Bush delivered a superb address to the joint session of Congress on Sept. 20, Kesey, watching from his living room in Pleasant Hill, Ore., shook his head in weary-eyed disgust. "Bush has just finished his big talk to Congress and the men in suits are telling us what the men in uniforms are going to do to the men in turbans if they don't turn over the men in hiding," he lamented. "The talk was planned to prepare us for war. It's going to get messy, everybody ruefully concedes. Nothing will ever be the same, everybody eventually declares. Then why does it all sound so familiar? So cozy and comfortable? Was it the row after row of dark blue suits, broken only by grim clusters of high-ranking uniforms all drizzling ribbons and medals? If everything has changed (as we all knew that it had on that first day) why does it all wear the same old outfits and say the same old words?"

Such sentiments were considered unpatriotic heresy in the early days of the war on terrorism. It was a time to proclaim "United We Stand," pin an American flag on your lapel and salute the commander in chief. Celebrity artists appeared on TV telethons to raise money for the victims of the attacks while liberals of every stripe swallowed hard and admitted that President Bush had exceeded their low expectations. But Kesey, like some stubborn old-growth redwood tree, refused to join their ranks. He was by trade and temperament a dissenter in time of war, always poised on the precipice of the abyss, thumbing his nose at authority and championing the individual: underdog over big government.

For Kesey—the iconoclastic artist—lived by a simple motto he clung to with the tenacity of a pit bull. The job of the writer, he said, is to kiss up to no one, "no matter how big and holy and white and tempting and powerful."

Social Issues in Literature

CHAPTER 2

One Flew over the Cuckoo's Nest and Mental Illness

Kesey's Realistic View of the World of the Insane

Janet R. Sutherland

Janet R. Sutherland was a teacher in the English Department of Interlake High School in Bellevue, Washington.

In the following viewpoint, Sutherland defends One Flew over the Cuckoo's Nest *against charges that it is obscene, racist, and immoral. Ken Kesey uses obscene language to symbolize that the patients in the mental hospital are being treated in an obscene manner, she argues, but the novel is not racist. In fact, one of Kesey's themes is that Chief Bromden's mental illness has been caused by racism toward Native Americans. Kesey is not advocating immorality, Sutherland contends, but rather suggesting that an unbalanced person may sometimes see truths that elude the sane.*

In the judgment of one recent patron of the Bellevue Public Schools, Ken Kesey's *One Flew Over the Cuckoo's Nest* is not a decent book for students to read or teachers to teach. While literary critics might be able to dismiss such pronouncements as simply untutored, public school people have to deal with them frequently and take them seriously, in the interest of preserving their right of access to literature and the student's right to read. It is in this context that I offer a defense of Kesey's novel against the charge that it is an improper and even evil book, fit only "to be burned."

An Accurate Portrayal

Ken Kesey's *One Flew Over the Cuckoo's Nest* is not obscene, racist, or immoral, although it does contain language and scenes which by common taste would be so considered. Like

Janet R. Sutherland, "A Defense of Ken Kesey's *One Flew over the Cuckoo's Nest*," *The English Journal*, vol. 61, no. 1, January 1972, pp. 28–31. Copyright © 1972 by the National Council of Teachers of English. Reproduced by permission.

all great literature, the book attempts to give an accurate picture of some part of the human condition, which is less than perfect. Kesey's book is set in a mental hospital; the language, attitudes, and habits of the inmates are typical of disturbed men whose already distorted world is being further systematically dehumanized by the ward nurse. The story is told in the first person through the eyes of an Indian whose health is gradually restored to him and to others through interaction with the robust new inmate McMurphy, a picaresque figure who is transformed into a tragic hero as he struggles to help the inmates' regain control of their lives. To charge that the book is obscene, racist, or immoral because it gives a realistic picture of the world of the insane is to demonstrate a lack of the minimum competency in understanding literature we expect of high school students. The charge also ignores the extent to which this novel does conform to the standards outlined in the guidelines for selection of instructional materials in the Bellevue schools.

Our students are taught that to understand the general meaning of a book, the reader has to take all the details into consideration. The theme emerges from a complex combination of scenes, characters, and action, often in conflict and often contradictory. To judge a book simply on a few passages which contain unconventional language or fantasies is missing the point. In the case of the Indian narrator, we are seeing and hearing at times the hallucinations typical of schizophrenia. Chief Bromden has been systematically ignored and abused all his life to the point of madness. It is no wonder that his consciousness is filled with horrors, obscene and otherwise. What Kesey is telling us, beyond giving us a realistic idea of the actual language of the asylum, is that what is being done to these people is an obscenity. When McMurphy comes upon the scene, it is as if his outrageous speech and action are the only possible answer to the vicious way in which the men's privacy and smallest efforts of will are being pried into and exploited and diminished. His profanity is a verbal manifestation of the indecencies they suffer, the only appropriate response to it, a foil which helps us to see its actual nature, and a means by which the scene is transformed into a world in which some tenderness and love are possible. Big Nurse speaks properly but does unspeakable things. McMurphy's speech is outrageous; he fights the profane with the super profane and moves beyond profanity to help the men create a new respect for themselves. He restores Harding's ability to face reality, gives Billy a sense of his manhood, and convinces Chief Bromden that he is indeed his actual six foot six, not a withered deaf mute.

If the reader is really sensitive to the specific language of the book, he will see how Kesey uses its subtle changes to signal changes in the Chief's state of mind. The fogged-in scenes are characterized by confusion and some description of the grossness of the asylum's inmates and black help. As Chief Bromden recovers his powers of perception, including his sad past and the scenes of white racism and war which has produced his state of alienation, the sentence structure and word choice change markedly. So also the emphasis on McMurphy's outward grossness shifts in the Chief's eyes to an apprehension of what he is suffering inwardly, to his deeds of kindness to the men, his complicated and puzzling deals, and his final decision to protect another man though he knows it means his doom. The Chief sees beyond McMurphy's outward geniality to the marks of anguish on his secret face.

Three Themes Explored

To understand the book, then, is to experience through this unique point of view the emergence of at least three themes which the book has in common with other major works of literature. First, there is the idea that we must look beyond appearances to judge reality. Just as the reader has to look beyond the typically racist language of the inmates to find in the

book as a whole a document of witness against the dehumanizing, sick effects of racism in our society, so Bromden has to
look beyond the perception of the world which limits his con-
cept of self. When the perception changes, he begins to see the
reality of his growth. Chief Bromden is sick from racism and
is made whole again when he learns to laugh in spite of it and
to realize his identity as an American Indian. Second, there is
the idea that fools and madmen have wisdom. Writers from
Shakespeare to Kesey have suggested that the world is sometimes so out of joint that it can only be seen from some perspective so different that it cuts through illusion to truth.
[King] Lear and Hamlet both experience a kind of madness
for this reason, madness in which it might be added, they too
abandon propriety of speech. (Polite language has hardly ever
been associated with madness in literature.) And through this
madness, in Kesey's book, the third theme emerges: the idea
that the bumbling fool may be transformed into a worker of
good deeds. McMurphy assumes almost the stature of the
typical quest hero at his death. The circumstances of his life
have required him to rise above the "lowness" of his original
station to become a deliverer, to give up his life for his friend.
The idea is that each human soul is worthy, and it is the genius of heroism to work transforming deeds which discover
the worthiness both in themselves and in other humble men.

The book, then, works through the eyes and action of
madmen to go from a vision of the world where all things are
profane to a vision of the world where all human things are
potentially sacred. Certainly teaching the book compels a dis-
cussion of obscenity, for it is impossible to understand it fully
without realizing that what people do to each other in cruelty
is the true obscenity, not shadow words. The book does not
teach profanity; it teaches that the world of the insane is full
of profanity. It does not teach racism; it clearly connects racism with cruelty and insanity. It does not teach immorality; it

Vincent Schiavelli (as Fredrickson), Jack Nicholson (as R.P. McMurphy), and others in a scene from the 1975 film adaptation of Ken Kesey's novel One Flew over the Cuckoo's Nest. *United Artists/Fantasy Films/The Kobal Collection/The Picture Desk, Inc.*

suggests that the fantasies of an unbalanced person are sensitive to a disruption of ordinary morality. . . .

Most students know very little about either the world of the mentally ill or the alienated condition of the American Indian. The detail of the book richly provides this information. The weaving of these details into this particular story moves the reader to deep sympathy with the Indian and much compassion for the inmates of his asylum. I think it is a profoundly humanizing book. . . .

Teaching *Cuckoo's Nest*

Kesey is a valid part of the world of American literature. His books, if not available in the library at our high school, would easily be found in any bookstore or book rack. The attempt to "protect" the students from his view of the world is in the first place futile: they like *One Flew Over the Cuckoo's Nest* and will read it anyway. Second, such an attempt would be stupid.

Why neglect the opportunity to provide a framework or reason in which such an admittedly difficult book can be read, discussed, and understood—unless we want to garner the doubtful honors attributable to playing the role of Big Nurse of education, and further alienate the young people we are attempting to communicate with?

I conclude with the description of one remarkable scene in Kesey's book: Patients are allowed to vote in weekly group meetings about policies which concern their welfare and entertainment. McMurphy has requested that though the regular TV watching time is in the evening, patients be allowed access to the TV during the daytime while the World Series is being played. Big Nurse does not like this assertation of individual will which will upset the daily routine, so she opposes McMurphy and then overrules the patients' affirmative vote on a technicality. In spite of her ruling McMurphy puts down his tasks and pulls his chair in front of the TV as the game broadcast begins. It is a battle of wills, and the patients watch to see who will win. Big Nurse pulls the great lever and cuts off the power. But McMurphy remains solidly there, in front of the TV, watching the empty screen. One by one the others join him, and soon they're all sitting there, "watching the gray screen just like we could see the baseball game clear as day," and Big Nurse is "ranting and screaming" behind them.

"If somebody'd of come in and took a look, men watching a blank TV, a fifty-year-old-woman hollering and squealing at the back of their heads about discipline and order and recriminations, they'd of thought the whole bunch was crazy as loons."

It is unfortunate that the patron who has lodged the objection to this book was so distracted by its alleged obscenity, racism, and immorality that he couldn't appreciate this scene. It has something to say about the need for authority to establish itself through reasonable, not arbitrary action. It also illustrates the utter futility of ever trying to get between a human being and anything he holds as dear as baseball.

Mcmurphy Helps Chief Bromden Regain His Sanity

Barry H. Leeds

*Barry H. Leeds is professor emeritus of English at Central Con-
necticut State University and the author of* The Enduring Vision of Norman Mailer.

*In the following essay Leeds contends that the lesson McMurphy
teaches his fellow inmates in* One Flew over the Cuckoo's Nest
*is that they will regain their manhood when they accept both re-
sponsibility for their own actions and responsibility for each
other. Chief Bromden learns this lesson. As McMurphy is eventually destroyed by the system, Bromden becomes stronger and
regains his sanity and manhood.*

Within a highly disciplined form, [Ken] Kesey has dealt
with issues which loom prominently in the minds of
those whose primary criterion for any idea or pursuit is its
"relevance." The questioning of a monolithic bureaucratic order, the rejection of stereotyped sexual roles, the simultaneous
awareness that healthy sexuality and a clear sense of sexual
identity are prerequisites for human emotional survival, the
recognition and rejection of hypocrisy, the devotion to the expression of individual identity: all these leap into sharp focus
through a study of Kesey's technique.

Even in Death, McMurphy Wins

Randle Patrick McMurphy, the protagonist of *One Flew Over
the Cuckoo's Nest*, is a man who has consistently resisted the
strictures of society. Having decided that life on a psychiatric

Barry H. Leeds, "*One Flew over the Cuckoo's Nest*: 'It's True Even If It Didn't
Happen,'" in *Ken Kesey*, Lynn, MA: Frederick Ungar Publishing Co., 1981, pp. 13–43.
Copyright © 1981 by Frederick Ungar Publishing Co. Inc. Republished with permission
of The Continuum International Publishing Company, conveyed through Copyright
Clearance Center, Inc.

ward will be preferable to hard labor on the county work farm where he has been serving a sentence for assault and battery, McMurphy feigns insanity. This brings him into dramatic confrontation with "Big Nurse," a representative of the most repressive aspects of American society. Big Nurse is backed by the power of a mechanistic "Combine," a central agency for that society's suppression of individuality.

During his stay on her ward, McMurphy fights a constant guerrilla action against Big Nurse and her aides. He rallies the other patients behind him as he introduces gambling, laughter, and human vitality to the ward. He leads the patients on a therapeutically rejuvenating deep-sea fishing trip. In a penultimate rebellion, he smuggles whores and liquor onto the ward for a hilarious party.

Against this humorous backdrop, the struggle between McMurphy and Big Nurse continues to escalate. In the climactic final scenes, she is able to provoke him into outbursts of violence which provide the excuse to "treat" McMurphy with electro shock therapy (EST) and ultimately with a lobotomy. In the moving conclusion, McMurphy's friend Chief Bromden mercifully smothers him to death and makes his own escape. Although McMurphy is ultimately destroyed, he is not defeated. His courage and humor are never broken. Even after his death, his spirit pervades the ward; it is clear that he has beaten Big Nurse and damaged the Combine.

It is not only McMurphy's own struggle which is at issue in this novel. For one thing, McMurphy comes to represent the only hope for salvation open to his fellow inmates, a salvation which he brings about through the tutelage of example, making them aware of their own manhood in the dual senses of masculinity and humanity. Also, the novel's first-person narrator, Chief Bromden, assumes during the course of the novel a rebel role similar to that of McMurphy. . . .

The progressive development of the characters of McMurphy and Bromden cannot be said to parallel one another; a more accurate geometric metaphor is that of two intersecting oblique lines: As McMurphy's strength wanes, Bromden's moves toward the ascendant. But the two developments proceed simultaneously and are integral to one another, until the transfer of power from McMurphy to Bromden is complete.

Bromden is an American Indian, a 280-pound, 6 foot 8 inch former high school football player and combat veteran of World War II who has been robbed of identity and sanity by the combination of pressures brought to bear on him by twentieth-century American society. At the outset of the novel, he is literally cut off from even the most rudimentary communication. He is so fearful of the dangers of dealing with people that he has learned to feign total deafness and has maintained absolute silence for years. Considered incurable by the medical staff, he is forced to perform menial janitorial work by the orderlies, who ridicule him with the title "Chief Broom."

The nickname has an obvious significance: Defined by his menial function, Bromden is no more than an object to the staff, a tool. But even his legal name, "Bromden," represents a false identity that is imposed upon him by others. Ironically, Chief Broom really is the son of a tribal chief, a once-powerful leader whose Indian name meant "The-Pine-That-Stands-Tallest-on-the-Mountain." "Bromden" is the maiden name of his mother, a white woman; and the fact that his father allowed himself to be henpecked into adopting it is invested with great significance by Kesey. The loss of pride in the Indian heritage brought about by the pressure of white American society (especially its matriarchal element, as represented by Mrs. Bromden) lies at the heart of the twentieth-century problem of Bromden, his father, and their people. The plight of the American Indian comes to represent, for Kesey, that of the American individualist in highly distilled form. The artificial identities of "Mr. Bromden" and "Chief Broom" imposed upon Bromden by the matriarchal and mechanistic elements of society diminish him enormously. The first robs him of his masculine pride and his racial identity, the second of his very humanity. Kesey forces us to abstract from this extreme case the realization that our own identities as self-determining individuals have been considerably eroded and are further threatened by a computerized civilization.

The experiences which have undermined Bromden's strength and sanity are revealed later in the novel in brief flashbacks, each precipitated by McMurphy as he persists in forcing Bromden to leave his fortress of silence and forgetfulness and reenter by stages the external world. As McMurphy makes friendly overtures toward him, Bromden begins to remember and understand episodes from his own past. In persistently attempting communication with Bromden, McMurphy functions as a sort of combination lay psychiatrist and confessor, precipitating more and more painful and traumatic memories out of Bromden's mind until the Chief is able to face his own problems and begin the trip back to manhood.

These flashbacks help establish for the reader an acceptance of Bromden as a sympathetic and fully developed character of considerable potential so that his later resurgence of power is both credible and emotionally charged. In addition, these passages are thematically useful to the author, introducing graphic substantiation of his central indictment of the Combine-controlled American society and its capacity to crush individuality and communication. Chief Broom is the tangible representation of the human alienation produced by the system. . . .

The Device of First-Person Narration

What is particularly impressive about *One Flew Over the Cuckoo's Nest* as a first novel is the highly credible integration of prose style and metaphorical patterns with the character of Bromden. Early in the book, Bromden's perceptions and the very rhythms of his speech are both informed and limited by his disturbed mental state. As he moves toward sanity and effective communication with others, Bromden perceives and articulates more clearly, and the prose style of the narrative reflects this development precisely. For example, fairly late in the novel, Bromden, who has been subject to frequent hallucination, takes the significant step of drawing a clear distinction between illusion and reality:

> There was little brown birds occasionally on the fence; when a puff of leaves would hit the fence the birds would fly off with the wind. It looked at first like the leaves were hitting the fence and turning into birds and flying away.

Bromden's hallucinations during the earlier part of the novel serve to establish and support the central aesthetic of the book, based on a fascinating subjectivity within which Kesey masterfully commands a suspension of disbelief. This is brought about largely through absolute candor on Bromden's part. He admits his own subjectivity and the extent of his alienation from our societal "reality," but in a crucial statement which sums up precisely the relationship between the rich metaphorical structure of his hallucinations and the central truths they elucidate, Bromden tells us (referring to the entire McMurphy story): "It's true even if it didn't happen."

Perhaps the most frightening product of Bromden's hallucinatory perception is the Combine itself. He defines it as a "huge organization that aims to adjust the Outside as well as the Big Nurse has the Inside." The Inside, as Bromden sees it, is different from the outside world only in the *degree* of control which must be exerted over its inhabitants. The Combine, committed as it is to the supremacy of technology over humanity, extends its influence by dehumanizing men and making them machines. But as the novel progresses, it becomes clear that Kesey envisions emasculation as a preliminary step in the dehumanization process. Ultimately, a pattern emerges: The Combine functions on two levels, mechanistic and matriarchal. The two are fused in the Big Nurse, Miss Ratched, who is a "high ranking official" of the Combine.

Big Nurse herself is conceived in mechanistic terms. Even her name, "Ratched," sounds like a kind of wrench or machine component, and the association with "rat" makes its very sound unpleasant. Bromden sees her as an expensive piece of precision-made machinery, marred in its functional design only by a pair of oversized breasts. Despite her annoyance at being forced to carry them, and despite Bromden's feeling that they mark an obvious flaw in an otherwise perfect piece of work, their presence is not inconsistent with the symbolic irony intended by Kesey. Miss Ratched's breasts are ironic reminders of the sexuality she has renounced. At the novel's end, they will be exposed by McMurphy as the palpable symbol of her vulnerability. Finally, they are her badge of membership in the Smothering Mother cadre of the Combine. . . .

Upon McMurphy's arrival at the ward, he tells the inmates that "the court ruled that I'm a psychopath. . . . Now they tell me a psychopath's a guy that fights too much and f----s too much. . . . " Although Kesey renders McMurphy's character in such a way that his sanity never seems questionable to the reader, it is significant that his cunning but unschooled ruse is so readily acceptable both to prison authorities and to the medical staff of the hospital. The central issue seems to be that the two areas in which McMurphy's animal vitality manifests itself, rage and sexual energy, form a two-pronged threat to the dual repressive roles of the Combine: mechanistic order and matriarchal emasculation. Having classified brawling and promiscuous sexual activity as "anti-social" forms of behavior, the authorities make the easy assumption that a man who sees such behavior as a desirable and valid form of life must be insane. . . .

Not Only Manhood but Also Humanity

Being a man is more than being physically strong or even courageous. It entails sensitivity and a commitment to other people, because manhood, as Kesey sees it, is not merely the quality of being male but of being human. What McMurphy teaches the inmates is not merely how to be aware and proud of their sexual identity but how to be human beings as well, responsible for one another. In the process, he himself develops greater maturity and responsibility, progressing from good-natured selfishness to a selfless commitment to his fellows. . . .

From the outset, McMurphy has been aware that guerrilla action is the method by which Big Nurse may be harassed safely. But as Miss Ratched, after losing a few hands, calmly continues to raise the stakes from behind her mechanical poker face, McMurphy is forced to choose between backing off and calling her bluff.

What keeps the contest from becoming either morbidly dull or unbearably terrifying to the reader is Kesey's capacity to render absurd humor. Toward the end of the book, Harding says of the farewell party for McMurphy, "It isn't happening. It's all a collaboration of [Franz] Kafka and Mark Twain. . . ." and one gets the idea that Kesey extends this judgment to the entire world of the Combine.

It is in this spirit of easygoing humor that McMurphy begins to break through Bromden's defenses and draw him back into the world. Although the central improvement in Bromden is psychological, its outward manifestations are tied to the metaphor of physical size and potency. When the partially reclaimed Bromden lies awake, anxious to go on the fishing trip, McMurphy talks to him and offers to make him "big" again. After listening to McMurphy describe the two whores who are coming on the trip, Bromden experiences his first erection in many years; and McMurphy, pulling back the blankets, bawdily puns, "look there, Chief. . . . You growed a half a foot already." The pun is significantly close to literal truth, for sexual potency is shown as both a symptom and a function of masculine identity; Bromden's new self-awareness will result in a fearsome potency which thwarts the Combine and its agents, combined with a commitment to his fellow inmates which spells hope for all men. . . .

Bromden Replaces McMurphy

The battle lines are drawn by the agents of the Combine; but instead of demoralizing the men, this pulls them closer together. In defense of another inmate, and with resignation rather than anger, McMurphy allows an orderly to goad him into a fistfight which he knows will provide Big Nurse the excuse she needs to bring more formidable weapons into play. Perhaps more significant is the fact that Bromden, accepting responsibility for his fellow man, steps in to help McMurphy when he is outnumbered.

From this point on, Bromden is his own man, growing in strength as McMurphy declines. The two go together to the EST [electroshock therapy] room. For Bromden, this shock treatment, his last ever, is a turning point. With McMurphy as an example, he fights his panic, takes his treatment, and then works his way back out of the fog, never to hide in it again. Bromden returns to the ward to be greeted as a hero by the other men, largely assuming McMurphy's former position, while McMurphy, the focus of Big Nurse's vengeance, undergoes repeated shock treatments.

With no end to the treatments in sight and Big Nurse considering more drastic methods, it is decided that McMurphy's escape from the hospital must be engineered. McMurphy agrees but insists on postponing his departure until after a secret midnight visit from Candy and her friend Sandy, which turns into a farewell party, fueled by cocktails made of codeine-based cough syrup and a few friendly tokes of marijuana with Mr. Turkle.

The party is a success on every level. Billy Bibbit loses his virginity to Candy in the seclusion room, the men draw closer together and begin to entertain hopes of overcoming the control of the Combine, and McMurphy's escape before dawn, using Turkle's key to unlock a window, is assured. Bromden articulates the full significance of the rebellion: "I had to keep reminding myself that it had *truly* happened, that we had made it happen. . . . Maybe the Combine wasn't all-powerful." But although they have in the past overestimated the strength of the Combine and Big Nurse, this time Bromden and the others have underestimated it. It is only McMurphy who still recognizes the extent of the control held over the men and understands the fact that his own complete sacrifice is necessary to effect their freedom. He decides to take a nap before leaving, "accidentally" oversleeps, and is discovered by the morning staff.

In retrospect, Bromden is able to understand McMurphy's motives and the inevitability of the events to follow:

> . . . it was bound to be and would have happened in one way or another . . . even if Mr. Turkle had got McMurphy . . . off the ward like was planned. . . . McMurphy would have . . . come back . . . he could [not] have . . . let the Big Nurse have the last move. . . . It was like he'd signed on for the whole game. . . .

When Billy Bibbit is discovered asleep in Candy's arms (a scene notable for its childlike innocence), Big Nurse proceeds to barrage him with recriminations until the old habit patterns of guilt and dependence are reawakened. Moments later, Billy commits suicide by cutting his throat.

Nurse Ratched's reaction is typical of her smug confidence in the infallibility of her own Combine-sanctioned values. She lays the blame immediately at McMurphy's feet. Bromden watches him

> . . . in his chair in the corner, resting a second before he came out for the next round. . . . The thing he was fighting, you couldn't whip it for good. All you could do was keep on whipping it, till you couldn't come out any more and somebody else had to take your place.

Bromden is the man who will take McMurphy's place, and because of this he understands what McMurphy must do. He is acting as an agent for all the men, and as Bromden realizes, "We couldn't stop him because we were the ones making him do it." In his final, physical attack on Nurse Ratched, McMurphy rips her starched uniform off, tearing down her insulation as he did with the glass wall, exposing her large, fleshy breasts, and making it clear that she is a vulnerable woman rather than an invincible machine. She will never again command absolute power over the inmates.

The aftermath is the complete disintegration of Miss Ratched's rule. Most of the men sign themselves out, but Bromden postpones his departure because he suspects that Big Nurse may make one last play. He is correct: One day, McMurphy, now a vegetable after undergoing a lobotomy (perhaps the ultimate castration), is wheeled back into the ward. In a scene characterized by an intense intimacy, Bromden performs a merciful service for McMurphy, smothering him to death. The transfer of power is complete. Bromden picks up McMurphy's hat, tries it on, and finds it too small. He feels "ashamed" at trying to wear it because he knows that McMurphy has taught him that one must find one's own identity. Then he picks up the control panel, smashes it through a window, and makes his escape.

Bromden is McMurphy's most successful disciple. It is not until the very end of the novel, however, that it becomes clear that Bromden has surpassed his teacher in the capacity to survive in American society and to maintain personal identity in spite of the Combine. It must be remembered that Bromden is a half-breed and that this mixed heritage has been a major contributing factor to his severe alienation and identity problems. But Bromden shows that his half-breed status also represents a capacity to combine the strengths of both the Indian and the white man. From his father he inherited a functional cunning, a patient caution which in its original form was conducive to both survival and pride. Although this quality has been perverted into the fearful "caginess" he once practiced and professed to admire, it is, in a less extreme form, a valuable attribute.

From the first page, it is clear that Bromden has long practiced the tactic of evasion against the onslaughts of the Combine. The price he has paid in loss of pride and identity obscures for a time the undeniable fact that he is the only man who has *fooled* the Combine successfully: Big Nurse and her staff believe that Bromden is a deaf-mute, and he is able to eavesdrop safely on their most private dealings. McMurphy, because he fights the Combine head-on, dies; but Bromden, who learns to practice a fusion of evasive cunning and sheer courage, survives as the hope for the future.

It is clear that one need not have the physical prowess of a McMurphy or a Bromden to renounce rabbithood and become a man. Kesey suggests that someone like Dale Harding has a very real chance to thwart the Combine, and even Billy Bibbit is able to go part of the way. Despite Billy's failure, Kesey's feeling is clear: It is better to be destroyed in the attempt to fight the Combine than to accept the role of rabbit for life.

Randle Patrick McMurphy is a compelling figure. Into the sterility of Bromden's world and the stifling American society it represents, he brings a breath, a breeze, a wind of change. In the wasteland of the ward, his sexual vitality makes him loom as a figure of mythic proportions. Yet the most important part of the legacy he has left Bromden and his fellows is that he was just a man. And that, finally, is enough.

The Patients in *Cuckoo's Nest* Regain Their Manhood by Banding Together

Terence Martin

Terence Martin is Distinguished Professor Emeritus in the Department of English at Indiana University. He served for two terms on the editorial board of the journal American Literature *and is on the board of the journal* Nineteenth-Century Literature. *He has published numerous works on literature, including* Parables of Possibility.

When McMurphy enters the mental hospital in One Flew over the Cuckoo's Nest, *it is a matriarchy, and the male inmates have been emasculated by Big Nurse and the other domineering women in the novel, according to Martin in the following essay. McMurphy represents freedom, possibility, masculinity, and brotherhood. Under his influence the inmates unite against the forces of control and regain their freedom.*

When Randle Patrick Mcmurphy swaggers into the cuckoo's nest, brash, boisterous, with heels ringing off the floor "like horseshoes," he commands the full attention of a world held crazily together in the name of adjustment by weakness, fear, and emasculating authority. As Chief Bromden says, "he sounds big." When, six weeks later, he hitches up his Moby Dick shorts for the final assault on the Big Nurse and walks across the floor so that "you could hear the iron in his bare heels ring sparks out of the tile," he dominates a world coming apart at the seams because of strength, courage, and emerging manhood. As Chief Bromden says (repeatedly)—he has made others big.

Terence Martin, "*One Flew over the Cuckoo's Nest* and the High Cost of Living," *Modern Fiction Studies*, vol. 19, no. 1, Spring 1973, pp. 53–55. Copyright © 1973 by Purdue Research Foundation, West Lafayette, IN 47907. All rights reserved. Reproduced by permission of The Johns Hopkins University.

The Mental Hospital Is a Matriarchy

The early McMurphy has a primitive energy, the natural expression of his individualism. And in the manner of the solitary hero his freedom and expansiveness come from being unencumbered. He has "no wife wanting new linoleum. No relatives pulling at him with watery old eyes. No one to *care* about, which is what makes him free enough to be a good con man." The later McMurphy, however, is thoroughly encumbered with the shrunken men on the ward, committed to a desperate struggle for *their* manhood—even though, as the Chief sees, "the thing he was fighting, you couldn't whip it for good. All you could do was keep on whipping it, till you couldn't come out any more and somebody else had to take your place." That kind of struggle, necessary, sacrificial, and fierce in its dedication, is what Ken Kesey dramatizes in *One Flew Over the Cuckoo's Nest* with an intensity of focus at once sanative and cleansing.

"We are victims of a matriarchy here," explains Harding to McMurphy: Doctor Spivey cannot fire the Big Nurse. The authority to hire and fire belongs to the supervisor of the hospital, a woman and an old friend of Miss Ratched's from Army days (the supervisor is anonymous, a virtual extension of the Big Nurse). It is McMurphy's first lesson in the ways of the madhouse. Women in the novel, one comes to see quickly, are powerful forces of control. They represent a sinister contemporary version of a feminist tradition in American literature that goes back, at least, to Dame Van Winkle [of Washington Irving's 1819 short story "Rip Van Winkle"] and that percolates through the popular fiction of the nineteenth-century in the form of domestic tyranny—as Helen Waite Papashvily has shown with her chapter "The Mutilation of the Male" in *All the Happy Endings*. Given the highly charged vision of *One Flew Over the Cuckoo's Nest*, female authority becomes nondomestic, hard, insistently emasculating.

Not all of the women are cast in the mould of the Big Nurse. Harding's wife, for example, is a bitch of the first order, whose visit to the hospital shows us all what Harding must overcome in himself as a prerequisite to overcoming something in her. . . .

In a different way Billy Bibbit's mother denies him the chance to become a man. A receptionist in the hospital, she is a neighbor and "dear personal friend" of the Big Nurse's; her hair "revolv[es] from blond to blue to black and back to blond again every few months." Billy, on a comfortable day, talks about looking for a wife and going to college. His mother tickles his ear with dandelion fluff and tells him he has "scads of time" left for such things. When Billy reminds her that he is thirty-one years old, she replies, "*Sweet*heart, do I look like the mother of a middle-aged man?" Again, the Chief has a final word: "She wrinkled her nose and opened her lips at him and made a kind of wet kissing sound in the air with her tongue, and I had to admit that she didn't look like a mother of any kind."

Chief Bromden, too, knows of female dominance. His Indian father took his white wife's name when they married and suffered a diminishment of self ever after. . . .

Only McMurphy stands outside such woman-power. His name . . . identifies him as the son of Murphy, not of Mrs. Murphy. . . .

Matriarchy in *One Flew Over the Cuckoo's Nest* comes, we see, to be expressed in various forms of female tyranny. It can sink Harding into the quicksands of inadequacy or make a Lilliputian [the tiny inhabitants of an island in Jonathan Swift's *Gulliver's Travels*] of the Chief's giant father. But its primary force and motive is to make men be little boys, to make them (want to) adjust to a role wherein lies safety. On the Disturbed Ward after the bruising fight with the orderlies, Chief Bromden notes the appearance of the Big Nurse: she "talks with McMurphy, soft and patient, about the irresponsible thing he did, the childish thing, throwing a tantrum like a little boy—aren't you *ashamed?*". If McMurphy—she calls him "Randle" at this point—will see his behavior in her terms, he will not be punished. When she finds Billy Bibbit with [the prostitute] Candy, she shatters his new-found sense of manhood by wondering how Billy's mother will take the news. Billy wilts immediately; stuttering once again, he disavows affection and friendship, and the Big Nurse leads him into the office, "stroking his bowed head and saying 'Poor little boy, poor little boy.'" After which Billy commits suicide, unable to become a man and be jerked back to boyhood all in the space of a few hours. . . .

In such a world McMurphy, the epitome of raw, unvarnished maleness, represents all the Big Nurse needs to control. As the contours of the narrative take form, the bigger-than-life McMurphy and the bigger-than-life Miss Ratched come to be opposed in every way. He is the stud, she the "ball-cutter"; he is the brawler, she the manufacturer of docility; he is the gambler, she the representative of the house—where chance has no meaning.

McMurphy Brings Laughter

The opposition between McMurphy and the Big Nurse goes to the very center of the novel, to the perception of Chief Bromden. Whenever the Big Nurse seems in indisputable control, the fog machine churns out its mist, scary, safe, and scary again. When McMurphy wins a skirmish, the fog disappears and the Chief sees clearly. . . .

As part of the Chief's mode of perception, the fog machine is a metaphor for tyranny, fear, and hiding which becomes literalized in his narrative. . . .

McMurphy's laughter and singing, his tall biographical tales, and the authentic ring of his idiom at once dominate the ward and define him to the other patients. His example, of course, evokes the choked off manhood of the men on the ward and a sense of freedom they have forgotten, or not known. When, later, McMurphy organizes the fishing expedition, it is a shared adventure, exciting, fun, and noisy. During one hectic, scrambling moment on the boat, with Candy's breast bruised and bleeding and the Chief's thumb smarting red from the line, McMurphy looks on and laughs—"because he knows you have to laugh at the things that hurt you just to keep yourself in balance, just to keep the world from running you plumb crazy. He knows there's a painful side . . .; but he won't let the pain blot out the humor no more'n he'll let the humor blot out the pain." Harding is laughing this time, and Scanlon, too, "at their own selves as well as at the rest of us." And Candy laughs, "and Sefelt and the doctor and all." The laughter

> started slow and pumped itself full, swelling the men bigger and bigger. I watched, part of them, laughing with them— and somehow not with them. I was off the boat, blown up off the water and skating the wind with those black birds, high above myself, and I could look down and see myself and the rest of the guys, see the boat rocking there in the middle of those diving birds, see McMurphy surrounded by his dozen people, and watch them, us, swinging a laughter that rang out on the water in ever-widening circles, farther and farther, until it crashed up on beaches all over the coast, on beaches all over all coasts, in wave after wave after wave.

Community laughter this, comic, aware, the signature of a deep experience, the expression of freedom—earned and shared. The fishing expedition, brilliantly handled by Kesey, accentuates the growing sense of community among the patients. It also contains the most joyous sounds in the novel. McMurphy, we know, has red hair, tattoos, and hands that bear the marks of work and combat. But his capacity for laughter is fundamental to his identity as a character—along with his ability to make us laugh. "That's clean enough," he says to the orderly watching him clean the urinals, "maybe not clean enough for some people, but myself I plan to piss in 'em, not eat lunch out of 'em."

The McMurphy who shakes hands with all of the men and announces himself as "bull goose looney" has much to learn about his new situation beyond the fact of matriarchal authority. He is, at first, what he has always been, the con man, the gambler in search of new territory; and he has managed to get himself committed to avoid the regimen of the work farm. Characteristically, he seizes the opportunity to bet on his ability to outmaneuver the Big Nurse. Surprised and disappointed when the patients do not support his motion to watch the World Series on TV, McMurphy again bets on himself, this time with a new purpose: his failure to lift the steel and cement control panel, foredoomed, according to the Chief, is an example of courage not lost upon the others. The next day they attempt the impossible and, as we have seen, reach their majority, twenty-one, in a second vote on the Series. (Interestingly, one of McMurphy's favorite games is blackjack, or twenty-one. Another, fittingly, is stud poker.) That they sit watching a blank screen, courtesy of Miss Ratched, gives their gesture an added, self-contained, significance; the cowboy-hero turned home-run hitter is now in their midst. They are now, as even the Big Nurse knows, a different group from the one they were before the advent of McMurphy.

McMurphy Learns Two Truths

McMurphy goes through two other stages in the course of the novel, both the result of increasing awareness. From the life-guard at the swimming pool he learns the difference between being *sentenced* and being *committed*. He realizes for the first time that he will be released only when the Big Nurse approves a release for him. The information has an immediate effect. As they are leaving the pool, a hydrocephalic [having an enlarged head due to too much fluid in the skull] patient from another ward lies helplessly on his side in the footbath,

Brad Dourif (as Billy Bibbit), Jack Nicholson (as R.P. McMurphy), Danny DeVito (as Martini), Vincent Schiavelli (as Fredrickson), Christopher Lloyd (as Taber), and others in a scene from the 1975 film adaptation of Ken Kesey's novel One Flew over the Cuckoo's Nest. *United Artists/Fantasy Films/The Kobal Collection/The Picture Desk, Inc.*

his head bobbing around in the disinfectant. Harding twice asks McMurphy to help him and Cheswick lift the boy up. "Let him lay," says McMurphy, as he walks on, "maybe he don't like deep water." The next morning McMurphy polishes the latrine "till it sparkled" and waxes the hall floors when asked to.

As the others recognize, McMurphy is playing the game, playing it safe—"getting cagey," the way "Papa finally did." At one time the Chief's father used to poke fun at the government men, speaking to them dead-pan like a stage Indian addressing tourists—to the great amusement of his Council. Like McMurphy, Chief Bromden's father learned to play it smart. The other patients on the ward understand about McMurphy; they are not angry or even disappointed. But there is a fearful cost to McMurphy's decision to think of Number One: Cheswick, who has achieved a certain momentum toward manhood, gets caught in the drain the next time they are at the swimming pool and drowns well before McMurphy, the lifeguard, and the orderlies can bring him to the surface.

McMurphy has one staggering fact left to learn. It astonishes him into meditative silence, then catapults him into his final role of savior. He hears from Harding that only a few of the patients on the ward, indeed, in the whole hospital, are committed. The great majority are there voluntarily, because, as Billy Bibbit says sobbingly, they don't have the guts to be Outside. The news is hardly credible to McMurphy. But his reaction to it is swift and thorough. At the ensuing Group Meeting he walks "big as a house" toward the Big Nurse, the "iron in his boot heels" cracking "lightning out of the tile," and rams his hand through the window in the front of her office as he reaches for his cigarettes. When a new glass is installed, he does it again. And when a third glass is put in, with a whitewashed X on it to make it clearly visible, Scanlon accidentally bounces a basketball through it before the whitewash is even dry.

Direct violations of the Big Nurse's private office, symbolic sexual assaults, are only the beginning. McMurphy, aware now of what *committed* means, aware, too, that the frightened men on the ward are there voluntarily, and aware, further, that he cannot defeat the Big Nurse and all that is behind her—even as he could not lift the control panel—begins to act for the others rather than for himself. Before McMurphy arrived, the patients were set against each other in the name of therapy and adjustment. Each man was a spy for the Big Nurse, eager to write down information about someone else in the log book near the Nurses' Station. In Group Therapy sessions they would peck at the victim of the day, currying favor by making one of their own miserable. McMurphy once says (apropos of the way in which Harding and his wife make each other impossible), "All I know is this: nobody's very big in the first place, and it looks to me like everybody spends their whole life tearing everybody else down." It is a central insight for the unsophisticated McMurphy—and one of the truest and most generally applicable statements in the novel.

During McMurphy's final stage things on the ward *begin* to change radically. Kesey, in masterful control of the fully activated materials in his novel, takes his madhouse men one last inevitable step, to an achieved sense of community. It is something he has consistently held dear: [Kesey's friend] Ken Babbs's "great statement," Kesey remarked in an interview in the *Rolling Stone*, was—"We don't want a commune, we want a community." Kesey's "great statement," made eight years before, was to turn a bunch of rabbits into a community of men, "close-knit," as [literary critic] Joseph J. Waldmeir observes, and "functioning." . . .

The men on the fishing trip and at the party are a far cry from the little boys who spied on each other and tattled in the Big Nurse's log book. No longer do they *tear* each other down. Before Harding signs out and is picked up by his wife, *he* deals blackjack in the tub room and tells the silent Big Nurse on her return, "Lady, I think you're full of so much bullshit." The language of the novel virtually insists that we see McMurphy as a kind of Christ figure (at Shock Therapy time: "Do I get a crown of thorns?" and earlier: "McMurphy led the twelve of us toward the ocean,"), doling out his life so that others may live. The action of the novel dramatizes the manner in which he makes his sacrifices, amid doubts and rejoicings on the part of his followers. And the perception of Chief Bromden, now highly sensitized to the task, prepares us at times tenderly to appreciate McMurphy's legacy—manhood, friendship suffused with affection, and, finally, love. Miss Ratched's face at the time of McMurphy's last attack displays a "terror forever ruining any other look she might ever try to use again." She has her revenge, lobotomy, a "castration of the frontal lobes." But Chief Bromden denies the Big Nurse her trophy. "He creeps into the bed of his friend," in the words of [critic]

Leslie A. Fiedler, "for what turns out to be an embrace—for only in a caricature of the act of love can he manage to kill him." It is, of course, as Mr. Fiedler signifies, a true act of love, performed with a manhood McMurphy has poured into the Chief.

In the terms of the narrative, there can be no more fog or time control. Thus, the Chief, bigger than ever before, makes his escape by picking up the control panel McMurphy could not even budge, the epitome of all the machinery in the hospital, of all machinery that has victimized him and diminished his people ("I heard the wires and connections tearing out of the floor"), and throws it through the window. . . .

McMurphy Brings Freedom and Space

On the trip to the ocean Chief Bromden notices "signs of what the Combine had accomplished since I was last through this country": five thousand houses "punched out identical by a machine," five thousand identically dressed kids playing on an acre of "crushed gravel," five thousand men deposited like insects by a commuter train. It is, recognizably, the world of our suburbs and sub-divisions, standardized, mechanized, virtually anesthetized. . . . The Combine, of course, continues to adjust things. But things may be increasingly adjusted (to pick up another idea from [critic Raymond] Olderman, who got it from McMurphy) because they are increasingly adjustable—which means, we realize with a sinking feeling of responsibility, that the Combine's power to control may exist in ratio to our willingness to forfeit manhood.

One Flew Over the Cuckoo's Nest directs our attention to such a point: we have surrendered a sense of self, which, for Kesey, is involved with a sense of space—and thus possibility. . . . To lose the *sense* of space is to be confined (whether it be on the Outside or on the Big Nurse's ward), to contribute to the encroaching power of the Combine.

And so Kesey gives us McMurphy, the advocate of our manhood, who brings a sense of space, freedom, and largeness onto the ward as something co-existent with his life. We hear him, we see him, and once we smell him—the outdoor odor of man working. . . .

The men on the Big Nurse's ward become stronger once they recognize their inter-dependence. McMurphy becomes heroic once he throws his lines out to them. And we come to appreciate the force of Kesey's novel once we see that *One Flew Over the Cuckoo's Nest* is an intense statement about the high cost of living—which we must be *big* enough to afford. That, I should think, is the "truth" the Chief speaks about at the outset. It will "burn" him to tell about it; it will "roar out" of him "like floodwaters." And it will remain true, for him and for all of us, "even though it didn't happen."

Mcmurphy Is a Psychopath, Not a Hero

Robert Forrey

Robert Forrey taught English at Shawnee State University in Ohio.

Forrey criticizes Terence Martin's article on One Flew over the Cuckoo's Nest *as overly generous to a sexist, lowbrow work of literature that mistakenly glorifies psychopathic behavior. Although Ken Kesey became a hero of the 1960s counterculture, he is actually a product of the 1950s, and he writes in the macho tradition of Ernest Hemingway and John Steinbeck, according to Forrey. The message that Kesey wants to convey in* One Flew over the Cuckoo's Nest *is that men need to free themselves from the emasculating influence of women. However, Forrey contends that this message is undercut by the repressed homosexuality manifested in the relationship between Chief Bromden and Randle McMurphy.*

Terence Martin's article on Ken Kesey's *One Flew Over the Cuckoo's Nest* ... seems to me to be part of an unfortunate trend among male critics to overpraise a novel which may be conservative, if not reactionary, politically; sexist, if not psychopathological, psychologically; and very low, if not downright lowbrow, in terms of the level of sensibility it reflects, a sensibility which has been influenced most strongly not by the Bible or a particular literary tradition as much as by comic books, particularly the Captain Marvel variety. Respectfully, but without the ritualized politeness that academic critics feel obliged to display when disagreeing with each

Robert Forrey, "Ken Kesey's Psychopathic Savior: A Rejoinder," *Modern Fiction Studies*, vol. 21, no. 2, Summer 1975, pp. 222–230. Copyright © 1975 by Purdue Research Foundation, West Lafayette, IN 47907. All rights reserved. Reproduced by permission of The Johns Hopkins University.

other, I would like to suggest a somewhat different interpretation of *One Flew Over the Cuckoo's Nest* than Mr. Martin and others have given us.

Based on 1950s Culture

Despite the fact that it became a favorite of the counter culture in the sixties, Kesey's *One Flew Over the Cuckoo's Nest* may actually be much more representative of the older, alcoholic, he-man, rather than the newer, drug, hippie culture. The values in Kesey's novel are not unlike those in the work of [Ernest] Hemingway and [John] Steinbeck. A high school wrestling champion in Oregon, Kesey came of age not in the sixties but in the fifties, when alcohol and tobacco were still the accepted drugs among young as well as old, when athletics and anti-communism were the chief preoccupations in American life, and when mothers were looked upon suspiciously as the castrators of sons and husbands. Like Hemingway and Steinbeck before him, Kesey presents as ideals in his first novel the arrogantly masculine ones of drinking, whoring, hunting, and gambling. Kesey is also in the tradition of Hemingway and Steinbeck in depicting his hero as a masculine Christ whom the conspiring world of weak-kneed men and bitchy women try to emasculate. In Hemingway and Steinbeck the Christ analogy is handled with a degree of restraint, but in Kesey it is unabashedly spelled out. Randall Patrick McMurphy's initials are not J. C., as with some of Steinbeck's feisty Christ figures, but he wears a crown of thorns and is crucified for his *machismo* far more explicitly than even Jim Casy [in Steinbeck's *The Grapes of Wrath*] or the fisherman Santiago [in Hemingway's *The Old Man and the Sea*].

The apparent menace to manhood in *One Flew Over* is the Combine, a vague and insidious ruling power which conspires against all who oppose it. The major symbol of the Combine is the machine and Kesey draws on two of the meanings of the noun "combine." A "combine" is, in informal usage, a group of people united for some monopolistic purpose; and also, of course, it is a harvesting machine. In choosing the machine as the central metaphor of oppression, Kesey follows a major literary tradition. As Leo Marx has shown [in *The Machine in the Garden*] the machine has long haunted the American imagination just as it has long blighted the American landscape. The machine is an appropriate symbol of the oppressive conformity and mechanical character of American life, for as [psychologist] Erik H. Erickson pointed out, when man over-identifies with his machines, he may want to become—and insist that everyone else become—machine-like, too. Almost always, however, the machine has been viewed as masculine in character. This makes sense because industrial society has been created by men. It is a man's world. But in his novel Kesey identifies the machine with the female. "Big Nurse," the villainess of *One Flew Over*, is a machine-like, castrating female. Her name, Ratched, means a toothed gear wheel in a threshing machine—i.e., a combine. McMurphy understands that the Big Nurse is not the solicitous mother figure she pretends to be but is "'a ball-cutter,'" "'tough as knife metal.'"

Emasculated by Women

Almost all the men in Kesey's imaginary mental hospital have been done in, if not actually committed by, women. Billy Bibbit, the stutterer, is a victim of his smothering mother. Harding, the sensitive intellectual, is a victim of his philandering wife. Broom Bromden, through whose schizophrenic stream of consciousness the story is told, is also a victim of women. His father, chief of the Columbia tribe, had stood proud and tall, but his white wife had cut him down just as she cut down her son. She did not even allow him to take his father's name; Bromden was *her* maiden name. Although the father had been tall and the son had stood six feet five, they were made to feel small by henpecking women. The government had wanted to build a hydroelectric dam on the Columbia tribe's land—a further encroachment of the machine. However, the government officials knew that the chief was too proud to sell out the birthright of his people for any price. At the suggestion of a scheming woman working for the government, the offer was sent not to the chief but to his white wife. Her greed was stronger than her husband's pride. "He fought it a long time till my mother made him too little to fight any more and he gave up," Broom recalled.

Women have robbed the men in the novel of their masculinity so that they are nothing more than an impotent brotherhood. "'There isn't a man here that isn't afraid he is losing or has already lost his whambam,'" Harding says, referring to their impotency. "'We comical little creatures can't even achieve masculinity . . . that's how weak we are.'" Harding blames it all on women. "'We are victims of a matriarchy,'" he says, "'and the doctor is just as helpless as we are.'" Although Kesey makes an attempt to qualify Harding's misogyny by suggesting that women are only representatives of the Combine, the fact is that it is women, not men, who run the Combine, just as it is women, not men, who really run the mental hospital. *One Flew Over* was written from the point of view that man's problems are caused by woman, who refuses to allow him to play the domineering role which nature intended him to play. The premise of the novel is that women ensnare, emasculate, and, in some cases, crucify men. The only good women in the novel are two whores who good-naturedly accept their role as sex objects and a Japanese nurse who is powerless to oppose the domineering bitches who control the men.

The Big Nurse is the biggest bitch. She pretends to be interested only in the welfare of the patients, but her real purposes are rather sinister. She refuses to allow the male patients to do anything which might remind them that they are still men. Not only does she forbid them to drink, whore, and gamble; she also rations their cigarettes and denies them the opportunity to watch the world series on television. All of these activities, as much as we may joke about them, have a sacramental value to males, or at least to red-blooded males, and no one understands their importance better than the randy hero of the novel, Randall Patrick McMurphy. By denying these sacraments of masculinity to the men, the Big Nurse succeeds in keeping them in line (at least until McMurphy arrives on the ward). Even the male doctor, who tends to sympathize with the male patients, is afraid of her because he is a drug addict who lives in fear of losing his job. The woman in charge of hiring and firing at the hospital is a good friend of the Big Nurse. Consequently, all the males on the hospital ward are under the Big Nurse's thumb, except perhaps for the black attendants who enjoy a special status. They work hand in glove with the Big Nurse against the white patients.

Since in the sixties the two major challenges to the rule of white American males came from blacks and women, it may be significant that the Big Nurse's closest allies are three black attendants. Specially picked and trained by her for their tasks, they are as cruel and sinister as those dark-skinned harpooners Ahab enlisted as accomplices to help kill the white whale, symbol of God and the phallus, according to some critics. The white whales on McMurphy's colorful underwear crudely underscore his identification with leviathan. If the Big Nurse seems intent on castrating the white male patients, the young black attendants seem equally determined to humiliate them sexually, either by taunting them verbally about their sexual inadequacies or by pulling down their pants and sticking needles, thermometers, or other objects up their rear ends. . . .

McMurphy Defies the System

Only when McMurphy arrives on the ward do the Big Nurse and her black attendants meet any opposition. A swashbuckling male, the Marlboro-smoking McMurphy challenges her because he has not yet been emasculated by women nor sexually intimidated by blacks. A bachelor and an ex-Marine who had fought in Korea, he has a devil with an M-1 rifle tattooed on one of his muscular shoulders and a poker hand tattooed on the other. Defying the tyranny of the Big Nurse as he had once defied his communist captors in a prison camp, McMurphy promotes gambling on the ward, organizes a basketball team among the patients, and undermines the authority of the Big Nurse in every way he can. Adapting Christian symbols and myths to his own novelistic purposes, Kesey characterizes McMurphy as a swaggering savior, a messiah of masculinity, erect and profane, shaking the matriarchal power structure. "McMurphy was a giant come out of the sky to save us from the Combine," Bromden believes.

When McMurphy first stands up against the Big Nurse at a group ward meeting, the other patients do not "stick up for their friend," to use the phrase from the novel, and McMurphy realizes that he has his work cut out for himself. He must raise them, as Christ raised the dead, for they are dead sexually. This means making them erect sexually, for in the novel the sexual organ is equated with the soul which the men cannot call their own. As Harding explains, the one weapon which men have against the "'juggernaut of modern matriarchy'" is their sexual organ, but every year "'more and more people are discovering how to render that weapon useless and conquer those who have hitherto been the conqueror.'" In seeking to restore the use of the sexual organ to the male patients, McMurphy runs a tremendous risk, a risk which is foreshadowed by the patient who is each day nailed to the wall of the ward by his sleeves. Only gradually does McMurphy become aware of the dangers involved in standing up for the other patients, but with a martyr's zeal he refuses to back down or give up his struggle, even after he knows the worst.

As part of his crusade to make the male patients men again, McMurphy plans a fishing trip for them, getting special permission for the excursion from hospital authorities. Of course McMurphy also plans to do some drinking and whoring with two prostitutes he has invited along, thus making it all a quintessentially masculine experience. . . .

McMurphy's efforts to uplift his fellow patients culminates in a late-night party on the ward, to which he invites the prostitutes. At the party the patients enjoy all the masculine prerogatives which the Big Nurse had deprived them of. And they enjoy them all night on the Big Nurse's own ward. As Bromden exclaims, "Drunk and running and laughing and carrying on with women square in the center of the Combine's most powerful stronghold!" Under McMurphy's inspiration and prodding, even Billy Bibbit, the stuttering mother's boy, manages to have sexual relations with one of the prostitutes. Unfortunately, they all drink themselves unconscious and are discovered the next morning—the prostitutes as well—by the day crew. The Big Nurse immediately tries to break up the spirit of brotherhood that the patients feel after the party. She tells Billy Bibbit that she will have to tell his mother how disgraceful he has behaved. Billy whiningly pleads with her not to tell his mother that he has spent the night with a prostitute. He blames what happened on McMurphy and the others, betraying the men with whom he had caroused the night before. Then like Judas, Billy goes off and kills himself, cutting his throat. "'I hope you're finally satisfied,'" the Big Nurse reprimands McMurphy, trying to discredit him in the eyes of the other patients. "'Playing with human lives—gambling with human lives—as if you thought yourself to be a God!'" In fact, it was the Big Nurse who was responsible for Billy's death, for she had made him feel guilty about his mother and then she had deliberately left him alone near the open medicine chest containing instruments with which he could kill himself. All McMurphy had done to Bibbit, according to the novel, was make him feel like a man for a night.

Enraged by the Big Nurse's accusation that he was responsible for Billy's death, McMurphy goes after her, crashing through the glass door to her office (as he had earlier crashed through the glass partition to recover his confiscated Marlboros) and rips open her uniform, exposing her breasts. This is possibly McMurphy's most important act in the novel, for in exposing her breasts, he is also exposing her womanhood which she had been so careful to keep hidden. She cannot expect to dominate the men unless she can make them forget she is a woman, and her large breasts were a constant reminder to them that she was. By exposing her breasts to the patients, McMurphy destroys her authority. . . .

Things go much too far to suit the Big Nurse. Through McMurphy's example, the patients have reached the point where they appear ready to stand on their own two feet. The Big Nurse retaliates with a drastic measure. Aware that electric shock treatments cannot break McMurphy's spirit, she manages to have him lobotomized. The operation turns him into a human vegetable, which the Big Nurse hopes will serve as a warning to his disciples. It is too late, however. The patients now know that she is just a woman—McMurphy had established that fact—and they begin to stand up for themselves. She had crucified their savior but she could not stop them—and the eleven of them leave the hospital or transfer from the ward. The towering Bromden no longer hunches all day in a corner. He escapes, but before he does he mercifully smothers the lobotomized McMurphy. Bromden's escape from the clutches of the Big Nurse is meant to carry great symbolic weight, for he represents the primitive male, the "Vanishing American," who was becoming a rare species. Ripping a machine up from the floor of the ward and tossing it out the window, Bromden makes his way to freedom and so, by extension, does the masculine spirit. The castrating Combine and the Big Nurses who run it have not been overthrown, but the eleven patients who escape will presumably keep McMurphy's lusty spirit alive, preaching the message that their oppressors are after all only women.

Repressed Homosexuality

One Flew Over the Cuckoo's Nest is one of a number of American novels of the last quarter of a century which have as their heroes psychopathic males who strike religious postures— prophets, saints, even saviors. Judging from Tom Wolfe's description of him in *The Electric Kool-Aid Acid Test*, Kesey himself seems to possess some of this religious megalomania. As a leader of the Merry Pranksters, Kesey acted so much like a religious prophet that some of his followers came to believe he actually was one. Wolfe himself writes *Electric Kool-Aid* in the spirit of the Gospels, as if Kesey were *the* one who led American youth out of the bondage of Middle America into the freedom of psychedelic-land. A groovy Unitarian minister saw Kesey that way, too. "Paul Sawyer looked at Kesey . . . and he saw a prophetic figure. . . . Somehow Kesey had created the prophetic *aura* itself, and through the Pranksters many people at the conference had not observed but experienced mystic brotherhood, albeit ever so bizarre . . . a miracle in seven days."

After Kesey was arrested for possession of drugs and faced a possible long jail sentence, he decided that the time had come to create the next step. He declared that the Hippie movement had to go beyond acid. A cynic might say that Kesey was simply trying to save his own skin and escape a jail sentence—which he did, or that he rides fads like a California surfer rides waves. However, in playing the prophet-Christ role he is not simply being a confidence man—although that may be part of it, just as it was part of McMurphy's role. Kesey actually sees himself as a kind of prophet or savior. When he turns up in *The Last Whole Earth Catalogue* recommending the Bible as the best defense against the evils of our industrialized world, he may be riding the ecological wave, but he is doing it again with the good book under his arm. But not everyone who believes in the Bible is necessarily doing the Lord's work. Many self-appointed prophets and saviors are simply mentally ill people who imagine they are unique victims of a conspiracy.

As [seminal psychiatrist Sigmund] Freud emphasized, feelings of paranoia and megalomania often stem from repressed homosexual impulses. *One Flew Over the Cuckoo's Nest* tries to suggest that this kind of psychoanalyzing is nonsense, that the problem is simply that men want to be men but women won't let them. Perhaps this is the case, but the thought persists that no psychologically informed reading of Kesey's novel can ignore the repressed homosexuality that seems to pervade it. Kesey himself was not unaware of this possibility, particularly in the relationship between McMurphy and Bromden which is presumably why the Indian at one point in the novel insists that his strong desire to touch McMurphy is not homosexually motivated. Perhaps Bromden is not latently homosexual. But if he and McMurphy and the other patients are, then what we have in Kesey's novel is yet another group of American males trying desperately to unite into a quasi-religious cult or brotherhood which will enable them to sublimate their homosexuality in violent athletic contests, gambling, or other forms of psychopathological horseplay. In recalling his first sexual relationship, at ten, with a nine-year-old girl. McMurphy affectionately calls her a "little whore"—"'Taught me to love, bless her sweet ass,'" by which he means of course not love in the Christian but in the sexual sense. Christ had warned that false prophets would come after him. We might add, so would psychopathic saviors. On the fishing trip, Mc-Murphy, the irrepressible prankster, tied two pieces of meat to the ends of a four foot string. Then he tossed it to two sea birds, who promptly swallowed the bait. "'Till death do them part,'" McMurphy wisecracked. It may be that those who think *One Flew Over the Cuckoo's Nest* one of the great novels of our time and McMurphy an indomitable culture hero, "the advocate of our manhood," in Terence Martin's phrase, have been similarly gulled.

Chief Bromden Conquers His Fears and Becomes a Hero

Annette Benert

Annette Benert is a professor of English in the Department of Humanities at DeSales University in Pennsylvania and the author of several works on literature, including The Architectural Imagination of Edith Wharton: Gender, Class, and Power in the Progressive Era.

One Flew Over the Cuckoo's Nest *addresses some central fears in twentieth-century America—fear of women, fear of blacks, and fear of machines—according to Annette Benert in the following selection. Benert points out that these fears are just fantasies. Chief Bromden and the other inmates need to come to terms with the fears that are within them in order to regain their sanity and their freedom.*

Ken Kesey dedicates *One Flew Over the Cuckoo's Nest* "To Vik Lovell who told me dragons did not exist, then led me to their lairs." It seems to me that Kesey does the same for us—and that the dragons are a special American breed and their lairs are in our own heads. The novel continues to compel an audience because it makes deep connections to several important strands of American psychic life—fear of woman, fear of the machine, and glorification of the hero who conquers both. The Terrible Mother of ancient mythology reappears as a frozen and fearsome Big Nurse, in imagery as transparent as the glass cage surrounding her. The Devouring Dragon has become the dynamo, the locomotive, the mad computer, the Combine—an all-powerful electronic presence

Annette Benert, "The Forces of Fear: Kesey's Anatomy of Insanity," *Lex et Scientia: The International Journal of Law and Science*, vol. 13, nos. 1–2, January–March 1977, pp. 22–26. Copyright © 1977 by Westminster Publications Inc. Reproduced by permission.

permeating the souls of men. Into this nightmare world comes the Savior, all red hair, libido, and cowboy bravado, whose reluctant heroism earns him an electronic crucifixion.

But the almost hypnotic power of the book's imagery should not blind us to another of its very American aspects. Intentionally or not, it is a tale told from a very special point of view, that of a man who, after all, has lived in mental hospitals for twenty years and who admits that "it's still hard for me to have a clear mind thinking on it." He has a cataclysmic nightmare about "crazy, horrible things too goofy and outlandish to cry about and too much true to laugh about." But, Bromden asks us, "if they don't exist, how can a man see them?"

He has no language to distinguish between literal and symbolic reality, empirical and psychic truth, but the power of his narrative derives largely from his ability to use what philosopher Susanne Langer calls "the essentially transformational nature of human understanding," making our "symbol-making function" one of our "primary activities, like eating, looking, or moving about," which "goes on all the time." What Chief Broom does naively, psychologists like Carl Jung do consciously, preferring to describe "the living processes of the psyche" in "dramatic, mythological" terms because they are "not only more expressive but also more exact than an abstract scientific terminology." Through Bromden's nightmare images, through what Jung would call his projections, we learn enough about one man's mind to make it a universe in which we too can live for a time. Correspondingly, his painful transcendence of the power and the glory he sees around him, his education into those qualities in himself, become our own.

This highly idiosyncratic voice is also universalized by yet another literary device, the unnamed narrator. His mother's name "Bromden" can never be adequate, and "Chief Broom" disguises his entire psychic reality, including his speech and hearing. As Billy Bibbit observes, "'he's scared of his own sh-

sh-shadow. Just a bi-big deaf Indian'"; in the words of Harding, he's "'a giant janitor. There's your Vanishing American, a six-foot-eight sweeping machine, scared of its own shadow.'" Hiding behind this anonymity is a man who scarcely felt it "possible that anybody could manage such an enormous thing as being what he was," who admires the maverick McMurphy's refusal to "let what he looked like run his life". The novel is thus also Bromden's account of his own struggle to transcend what *he* looked like—a big wooden Indian—and to become what he essentially is.

Like everyone else in the hospital—both patients and staff alike—what Bromden must primarily come to terms with is his own fear—fear of women, fear of blacks, fear of machines. All of these function as the fear of unused psychic possibilities: every man among them is scared of his shadow. A "whine of fear" hovers over a ward filled with "'the *rabbits*, one might say, of the rabbit world,'" who are "'even scared to open up and *laugh*.'" Their fearful faces make McMurphy also afraid, but they force on him a courageous posture that becomes increasingly grotesque. He can tell us the way out, tell us to try our fearfulness against what we fear, but he does not show us. The entire system of fear—of those who are driven by it and those who exploit it—combines to destroy him.

The task of showing is left to Chief Broom, and indeed we are given the complete reckoning only of his private misery and eventual salvation. His feigned deaf-muteness he has picked up like the invisibility of Ralph Ellison's character [in his book *Invisible Man*], because "it was people that first started acting like I was too dumb to hear or see or say anything at all." Though the mask has social origins, the pain behind it has deeper and more individual roots. His childhood memories are filled with his father—living in his adobe house, hunting with him, watching the tribe spear salmon over the falls, eating ants because "good Injun boy should know how to survive on anything he can eat that won't eat him first." "'My

Papa was a full Chief and his name was Tee Ah Millatoona. That means The-Pine-That-Stands-Tallest-on-the-Mountain, and we didn't live on a mountain.'"

Into this Edenic life intrudes—once again, in an archetypal American way—a massive hydroelectric power installation that destroys the Indians' village, means of livelihood, and tribal structure, at one stroke. As [critic] Leo Marx has documented in earlier American writers, one has "the sense of the machine as a sudden, shocking intruder upon a fantasy of idyllic satisfaction." The Eve in this garden is the white woman whom the Chief married and who brought with her the fancy dresses and the civilized ways that made her vulnerable to the big government bribe. And it is "an old white-haired woman in an outfit so stiff and heavy it must be armor plate" who knows that "'there is generally one person in every situation you must never underestimate the power *of*.'" What the boy witnesses, then, is a father who "'was real big when I was a kid'" and a mother who "'got bigger all the time, . . . bigger than Papa and me together.'" Finally, Bromden's once gigantic father just drinks from a bottle which "'sucks out of him until he's shrunk so wrinkled and yellow even the dogs don't know him.'" Naturally enough, "when I saw my Papa start getting scared of things, I got scared too."

Bromden consistently uses this metaphor of size to indicate both psychic power and, conversely, his own fear. "I was a whole lot bigger in those days," he recalls of an incident in high school: "'I used to be big, but not no more.'" He sees McMurphy as "'lot bigger, tougher'n I am,'" proving to his friend that "'you *are* crazy. . . . I swear you're the biggest Indian I ever saw.'" In the hospital swimming pool "McMurphy must of been standing in a hole because he was having to tread water where I was just standing on the bottom." A black aide sneers that Bromden is "big enough to eat apples off my head an' he mine me like a baby.'"

Miss Ratched, on the other hand, is "too big to be beaten. She covers one whole side of the room like a Jap statue." Mc-Murphy recognizes her as "just a bitter, icy-hearted old woman," but to Bromden she is the incarnate fusion of all his fears of women and machines. She seems a machine impervious to others, destructive in her force, omnipotent in her control. Her face is "white enamel," her nailpolish "like the tip of a soldering iron." Her hand bag is a "tool box" filled with "wheels and gears, cogs polished to a hard glitter, tiny pills that gleam like porcelain, needles, forceps, watchmakers pliers, rolls of copper wire." When she becomes angry, she "swells" up and her arms "section out" as she becomes "big as a tractor." She smiles "like a radiator grill" and smells of "hot oil and magneto spark." Most important, she controls the other machines, real and imaginary—the fog machines, the clocks, the radio, the television, the tape recorder in the wall, the magnets in the floor, the microphone in Bromden's broom handle, the gears and tubes and jumbled machinery in everybody else, which she checks with X-rays once a month. She controls, she shrinks, she freezes everyone in her path not because she is a monster machine, however, but because she "recognizes . . . fear and knows how to put it to use."

Working for her are an assortment of black men who "got special sensitive equipment [which] detects my fear"; when the smallest of them in particular "sucks in fear from all over the ward," Bromden, like a bluetick hound lost in the fog, "picks up no scent but his own fear." The blacks emit a "hum of black machinery, humming hate and death and other hospital secrets." They are "all of them black as telephones" with uniforms "white and cold and stiff as her own" and like her radiate frost. Around rebellious patients their arms are "bands of black iron," and in the showdown with them Bromden easily tosses one into the shower—"he was full of tubes: he didn't weigh more'n ten or fifteen pounds." Even more clearly than the Big Nurse, however, these men are not driven by wires and cogs but by "a high-voltage wave length of hate." They have been carefully handpicked because they "hate enough."

But Bromden seems to be even more afraid of machines than he is of women or blacks, perhaps because they are closer to his own inner reality. In the long nightmare sequence there are no women, no blacks—only "a huge room of endless machines stretching clear out of sight" like "the inside of a tremendous dam. Huge brass tubes disappear upward in the dark. Wires run to transformers out of sight. Grease and cinders catch on everything." As the dorm room slides down and out into this underworld landscape, the worker who comes with the meathook for a dead inmate has a "face handsome and brutal and waxy like a mask, wanting nothing." Later it is "Public Relation" with "half a dozen withered objects tied by the hair like scalps" to his stays who emerges out of the fog— again, a white man, the decayed remnant of the terrible power symbolized by the hydroelectric power plant. The dam, not the nurse—or, to use an inversion of Henry Adams' terms, "the dynamo," not "the Virgin"—lies at the core of Bromden's self, a core so powerful, so fear-inspiring, that he can touch it only through crazy fantasies and nightmares.

We have a quieter glimpse of this ambivalance toward the machine in the library, where Bromden looks "at the titles of books on electronics, books I recognize from that year I went to college; I remember inside the books are full of schematic drawings and equations and theories—hard, sure, safe things. I want to look at one of the books, but I'm scared to." He fears, then, not only what he is but what he has lost, both the power of technology and also its definiteness, its order, what [literary critic] Thomas Reed West calls its energy and its discipline.

Thus, the objective evil—and it is there—in Big Nurse, her black helpers, and the technology of psychological and environmental "adjustment" is overshadowed by the way Bromden has worked them all into the scenario of his own private

Will Sampson (as Chief Bromden) in the 1975 film adaptation of Ken Kesey's novel One Flew over the Cuckoo's Nest. © Photos 12/Alamy.

nightmare. Enough evidence sifts in from the corners of the novel to indicate that we are not to take any of the three as absolute evils in themselves. "The little Jap Nurse from Disturbed" implies that women in power are not always totalitarian; Mr. Turkle shows, if feebly, that black aides are not always sadistic; and the wild ride over land and sea—by car and by boat—demonstrates that modern technology can be freeing as well as enslaving, can bring man and nature, man and his own nature, together as well as force them apart.

We also have the varied perceptions of the other characters to remind us that Bromden's reality is not the only one. When Harding declaims about "'modern matriarchy'" McMurphy interrupts with "'Lord, Harding, but you do come on'"; Mrs. Harding may be a bitch, but "'you didn't make her feel like any queen either.'" When someone suggests that "'all single nurses should be fired after they reach thirty-five'" McMurphy amends, "At least all single *Army* nurses." Likewise, Harding explains to McMurphy that shock therapy "'isn't always used for punitive measures, as our nurse uses it, and it isn't pure sadism on the staff's part, either'"; in fact, even radical surgery has helped a few individuals. Together they help to remind Bromden—and us—that the real trouble is within.

Women, blacks, and machines have power over these men because they are given it, because, in the language of analytical psychology, it is projected onto them by the unlived femininity, or animal cunning, or power drives of the inmates. Bromden in particular projects so much because his conscious life, like his body image, has atrophied to a small fraction of what he is.

By the same psychic logic, the heroic qualities in McMurphy function primarily as they are projected upon him by the other men. We have already seen how Bromden perceives him as larger then he is. "He's broad as Papa was tall" and can "shrink" the Big Nurse from a "Jimmy Diesel" to "about head-high to where that towel covers him." To Bromden he "was a giant come out of the sky to save us from the Combine that was networking the land with copper wire and crystal," a man whose first handshake made Bromden's arm ring "with blood and power. It blowed up near as big as his." On the trip to the coast he made everyone feel "cocky as fighting roosters," showing us "what a little bravado and courage could accomplish."

Such an inflated image is easily turned against him. When Miss Ratched impugns his motives by pointing out how much money he has won from the other inmates, that image flips and the men can see, for a time, only the gambling shadow. Like the blacks with their nightmare faces, he is seen in negative. More important, the nurse knows that "'he isn't extraordinary. He is simply a man and no more, and is subject to all the fears and all the cowardice and all the timidity that any other man is subject to,'" though she does not understand what that means for his particular case. And in believing that "'he's much too fond of a Mr. Randle Patrick McMurphy to subject him to any needless danger'" she demonstrates her profound ignorance of the dynamics of her wardful of men. She underestimates both the men's need of his heroism and his own need to fill it. She underestimates what only Bromden seems really to understand—the power of human imagination.

Only Chief Broom seems aware of McMurphy's human weaknesses and of the way he is forced to live beyond them. During one man's seizure, he notices that McMurphy's face took on "that same haggard, puzzled look of pressure that the face on the floor has." Another man playing with the hydrotherapy equipment hallucinates victims in the canvas straps and tells McMurphy that "'they need you to see thum'"—and, indeed, he apparently has no choice. On the ride back from the coast, as McMurphy continues to dole out his life "for us to live," Bromden catches a glimpse of his real face, "dreadfully tired and strained and *frantic*, like there wasn't enough time left for something he had to do." Someone who had stayed behind "asked how come McMurphy looked so beat and worn out where the rest of us looked red-cheeked and still full of excitement." McMurphy turns to defend an inmate from the blacks with a voice "somehow sounding more tired than mad," a voice in which "everybody could hear the helpless, cornered despair." When the big party on the ward is over, McMurphy has "that strange, tired expression on his face again." The climactic battle with the Big Nurse is simply a "hard duty that finally just had to be done"; he then cries out with "a sound of cornered-animal fear and hate and surrender and defiance."

When Bromden returns to the ward after his own last bout with shock therapy, he feels forced to grin back at the men, "realizing how McMurphy must've felt these months with these faces screaming up at him." Harding recognizes that it wasn't "'the great, deadly, pointing forefinger of society'" that would drive McMurphy down their common road, but "'it is us.'" Watching McMurphy go into his last act, Bromden knows that "we couldn't stop him because we were the ones making him do it," impelling him "like one of those moving-picture zombies, obeying orders beamed at him from forty masters." Indeed, "it was us that had been making him go on for weeks."

Bromden and the rest so desperately need McMurphy to embody their own unlived lives, their own imaginative possibilities, that they force him to truncate his personality and, finally, to enact an electronic martyrdom, an act redemptive only in the sense that it points away from their own fears. McMurphy couldn't lift the control panel, and he couldn't save Cheswick's life, or Billy's, or even his own. "'But I tried, though. . . . Goddammit, I sure as hell did that much, now, didn't I?'" To "try" perhaps means to test one's fears against something solid, finding out, in the words of Walt Kelly's [comic strip character] Pogo, that "we have met the enemy and he is us." For Bromden to "try" seems to be to turn those eyes, which have seen so much of the inner world to which the others are blind, toward the outer world of objects and people, to allow himself neither to overestimate the one world nor to underestimate the other.

McMurphy's advent put Bromden in touch with his own mute mask in a new way and perhaps helped to catalyze that final nightmare. Then, through the fog that rolls in the next day Bromden understands for the first time that the old Chronics make "a sense of . . . [their] own," while Billy Bibbit reaches out "like the face of a begger, needing so much more'n anybody can give." Later a face up on Disturbed becomes "just a yellow, starved need," leading him to wonder "how McMurphy slept, plagued by a hundred faces like that, or two hundred, or a thousand." Parallel to Bromden's return to his rightful "size" and his new ability to fight his way out of the fog, even after electroshock, is a heightened capacity to see other people, to penetrate the fog and the masks into the fear and pain behind them.

"One night I was even able to see out the windows," relates Bromden. What he sees is a dog sniffing digger squirrel holes and a goose leading a flock, cruciform as he crosses the moon—a vision of himself and McMurphy perhaps, a symbolic fusion of the actual and the imagined that promises the integration of Bromden's world and Bromden's psyche. We see McMurphy repeatedly crucified on the shock table and deprived first of psychic and then of physical life as he leads his flock across the moon, through lunacy, over the cuckoo's nest. Then we see Bromden, not colliding with the car, as that dog may have, but declaring his own power over the Combine as he hurls the control panel out the window and flies away. Yet it is neither the destruction of the woman nor the destruction of the machine that has any final importance. It is rather Bromden's declaration of his own true nature, his own power, a power no longer trapped in destructive fantasies and projections, a power which is now his to use. As he declares at the end of the first chapter, "It's the truth even if it didn't happen."

One Flew over the Cuckoo's Nest Questions the Meaning of Sanity

Ellen Herrenkohl

Ellen Herrenkohl is a clinical psychologist in Bethlehem, Pennsylvania.

In the following essay Herrenkohl finds that in One Flew over the Cuckoo's Nest *Ken Kesey depicts two conflicts—the battle between the forces of conformity and individuality in society and the struggle within an individual to regain sanity by accepting personal responsibility. Initially, the inmates are as culpable as the mental institution, for they have ceded all control to the system. It is only when McMurphy teaches them that they have free will that they exercise it and regain freedom and sanity.*

Chronic schizophrenics are "machines with flaws inside that can't be repaired, flaws born in, or flaws beat in," Chief Bromden tells us early in *One Flew over the Cuckoo's Nest*. His definition reflects the resignation of patients and staff to a belief in individual helplessness and powerlessness. The entrance of McMurphy into the hospital scene sets the stage for the struggle between a resignation to external control and a striving for the stamp of individual control. The novel contains two dramas within this theme: the external struggle of the individual against the insanity of a machine-like environment in which he is caught; and the internal struggle of the individual for sanity through achieving a sense of personal reality. McMurphy dies as the hero of the former; Chief Bromden is reborn as the hero of the latter. It is this second drama that I shall focus on [here].

Ellen Herrenkohl, "Regaining Freedom: Sanity in Insane Places," *Lex et Scientia: The International Journal of Law and Science*, vol. 13, nos. 1–2, January–March 1977, pp. 42–44. Copyright © 1977 by Westminster Publications Inc. Reproduced by permission.

Inmates Systematically Dehumanized

The "institution" communicates and reinforces the notion of individual powerlessness in several ways. First, there is the stripping, literally and figuratively, of privacy and individuality. The "admission rites" to the ward include the subjection of the new inmate to the required shower: "The black boys come sign for him . . . and leave him shivering with the door open while they all three run grinning up and down the halls looking for the Vaseline." The "log book" is the loudspeaker for any personal information which leaks into the "therapeutic atmosphere" of the ward. "Talk," says the doctor, "discuss, confess. And if you hear a friend say something during the course of your everyday conversation, then list it in the log book for the staff to see. . . . Bring these old sins into the open where they can be washed by the sight of all. . . . There should be no need for secrets among friends."

The desire to be alone is seen as "sick." The nurses sit behind their glass wall and watch every movement of the patients in their therapeutic fishbowl. Nurse Ratched capitalizes on the phenomenon. [German social psychologist] Erich Fromm depicts as a central ailment of modern society: the loss of personal identity which makes conformity a necessity as one substitutes the expectations of others for the deteriorating sense of one's own standards and goals. She preaches the therapeutic necessity of togetherness: "'The doctor and I believe that every minute spent in the company of others, with some exceptions, is therapeutic, while every minute spent brooding alone only increases your separation.'"

The patients are robbed not only of privacy but also of maturity. Nurse Ratched calls her patients "boys" and addresses each as if he were "nothing but a three-year-old." Childlike helplessness is dictated at every turn by the staff. Routines are enforced at all costs. Only patient Taber has dared to ask the nature of the medication he is required to swallow and thereby has set himself up for a further lesson in enforced helplessness through lobotomy. McMurphy is "sentenced" to an undetermined number of months or years on the ward much as a child is banished to his room for misbehavior by an arbitrary authority figure.

The label of "insanity" is used to prejudice the meaning of human behavior. "Motivation" is seen to be limited to the self-centered drives of immature and unsocialized beings or the incomprehensible drives of insanity. When the naive Nurse Flinn asks Big Nurse why a man would seek to disrupt the ward, she gets this reply: "'You seem to forget, *Miss* Flinn, that this is an institution for the insane.'" Even laughter is taken to be the outbreak of an irrational, uncontrollable, and therefore undesirable symptom.

The ultimate lesson in dehumanization is the "invisible treatment." Not only are the patients treated as if they lack private history, meaningful behavior, maturity, and ability to reason, but they are even responded to as if they lacked material substance. Chief Bromden pushes his broom through the rooms and halls, unnoticed: "they see right through me like I wasn't there—the only thing they'd miss if I didn't show up would be the sponge and the water bucket floating around."

Sane People May Appear Insane

"Real Life" provides a recent analogue to Chief Bromden's fictional situation. In an experiment conducted by D.L. Rosenhan, eight sane people gained secret admission to mental hospitals in five different states by posing as psychotics. The experiment raised strong questions about the meaning of the term "insanity." After an initial complaint at the admissions desk about "hearing voices," each pseudopatient ceased pretending any symptoms of psychosis during his hospitalization. Yet, not one was detected as sane by the staff and each was discharged with a diagnosis of "schizophrenia in remission." The power of the label was such that innocent behavior, even note-taking, was viewed by the staff as pathological. Interestingly, Rosenhan, who himself participated in the experiment, confesses to having experienced the same sensation of invisibility which Chief Bromden describes: "A nurse unbuttoned her uniform to adjust her brassiere in the presence of an entire ward of viewing men. One did not have the sense she was being seductive. Rather, she didn't notice us. A group of staff persons might point to a patient in the dayroom and discuss him animatedly, as if he were not there." Kesey's "fiction" assumed a reality of bizarre proportions in this factual study. We are forced by Kesey to ask the same question that Rosenhan has asked: "How many patients might be 'sane' outside the psychiatric hospital but seem insane in it—not because craziness resides in them, as it were, but because they are responding to a bizarre setting" in which emotional avoidance, physical mistreatment, and psychological abuse depersonalize patients.

The Victims Share Some Blame

The institution has its methods of dehumanizing and deindividuating, but its victims are not without some share of the blame. The patients in Kesey's novel contribute to the process of dehumanization. First, they are eager to view themselves as controlled by forces beyond human control. They behave as if they have been committed and as if the duration of their "sentence" is up to the decision of the authorities. To McMurphy's amazement, it turns out that most of them are there because they have sought admission, and are too frightened to leave.

The "fog," which rolls in and descends on Chief Bromden encapsulating him and making motion difficult and vision unclear, is in actuality a barrier which he pulls down around himself to protect himself and create a cave of safety. The boredom from which he suffers is a symptom, not of disease, but of a deficiency in his own sense of control. Time comes to a dead stop and "freezes" or inches by, controlled, in Chief

Bromden's view, not by his own unwillingness to involve himself in the external world, but by the movement of others.
Chief Bromden eventually, however, comes to the realization
that his invisibility has been in part a product of his own
making, and that others begin to act as if he could not hear in
part because he behaves as if he did not hear.

Blaming genetic inheritance is another form of eager resignation to external control. "'I was born dead. . . . I can't help
it. I was born a miscarriage,'" cries Bancini. "'I was born a
rabbit,'" states Harding, hoping to defend his role of passivity,
and to blame his fear on the "'law of the natural world. . . .
We mustn't be ashamed of our behavior; it's the way we little
animals were meant to behave.'" McMurphy, of course, sees
that blaming inheritance is mostly self-deception.

The "victims" of the Combine are not only the hospital
patients, but the hospital staff as well, the authority figures
who run the machinery and monitor its dehumanizing process. The dehumanizing rules they enforce serve to dehuman-
ize themselves as well by providing them with a defense against
recognition of their own individuality, emotionally, and sexuality. There are many examples: the young nurse's embarrass-
ment at McMurphy's provocative teasing; Dr. Spivey's frightened lack of manhood; Big Nurse's attempt to rise above sex
and human warmth.

Free Will Is Necessary to Sanity

What is the safety that the fog and boredom and prisoner
mentality provide? Against what does the adherence and submission to helplessness protect its victims? Chief Bromden
grasps the meaning of the fog. McMurphy, he tells us, "keeps
trying to drag us out of the fog, out in the open where we'd
be easy to get at." To see clearly, to be seen clearly, is to be vulnerable. To admit to oneself one's feelings and one's perceptions is to be open to disappointment, to fear, to rejection, to
rage, to guilt, to tragedy.

McMurphy pulls Chief Bromden and his fellow patients out of the timeless fog in which they are submerged by assuming that men *do* have choices in life. This con artist assumes that Chief Bromden's deaf-dumb posture is a conscious pose. From the beginning "he wasn't fooled for one minute by my deaf-and-dumb act; it didn't make any difference *how* cagey the act was, he was onto me and was laughing and winking to let me know it."

The uneducated McMurphy understands the meaningfulness of "crazy" behavior. Insanity is not an explanation of anything for him, a dead-end label, an excuse. To be crazy is to be not without sense, but without guts. Chief Bromden comes to share McMurphy's point of view. Colonel Matterson, who began spouting "crazy talk" six years earlier, suddenly takes on a new dimension for Chief Bromden: "'I never paid him any mind, figured he was no more than a talking statue, a thing made out of bone and arthritis, rambling on and on with these goofy definitions of his that didn't make a lick of sense. Now, at last, I see what he's saying. . . . You're making sense, old man, a sense of your own.'"

In a supremely ironic twist, McMurphy the psychopath, the manipulator without a conscience, gives the inmates back their capacity for feeling guilt; for guilt is not possible without a sense of having chosen, of having decided, without a sense of freedom. McMurphy castigates the Acutes for cowardice, rather than excuses them because of illness. "'I ain't so sure but what they should be ashamed,'" he rages. His rage is based on the assumption that the patients are responsible men.

What do we gain with acceptance of responsibility and of vulnerability? Chief Bromden lets us in on the discovery in his climb out of the fog. One night, when "for the first time in years I was seeing people with none of that black outline they used to have," he slid out of bed. "I felt the tile with my feet and wondered how many times, how many thousand times, had I run a mop over this same tile floor and never felt it at all. . . . I smelled the breeze." Chief Bromden then suddenly finds himself in touch with childhood memories which had been previously lost in the fog. The reborn narrator sees and smells and feels and remembers, recapturing a sense of personal reality.

Chief Bromden thus reaches instinctively for the Frommian insight that man "would be free to act according to his own will, if he knew what he wanted, thought, and felt." Chief Bromden prepares, by reaching back inside himself, to touch base with his yearnings and his wounds. He is ready to accomplish what Fromm calls "man's main task in life": "to give birth to himself, to become what he potentially is." Bromden is the hero of the second drama of the novel precisely because he emerges with the necessary condition of sanity—a sense of personal identity.

The Insane Are More Rational than the Sane

Barbara Tepa Lupack

Barbara Tepa Lupack was an academic dean at the State University of New York and a Fulbright Professor of American Literature in Poland and France. With Alan Lupack, she is the coauthor of King Arthur in America.

It is the first-person, hallucinatory narration by Chief Bromden, a schizophrenic and mute American Indian, that gives One Flew over the Cuckoo's Nest *its emotional impact, contends Lupack in the following selection. The inspiration to make the chief narrator came to Ken Kesey while he was under the influence of the drug peyote. At the beginning of the novel, the chief appears to be one of the most severely damaged cases on the ward. Under McMurphy's influence, he gradually regains his sanity, and his narrative becomes less surreal. At the end, McMurphy is sacrificed, but the men regain control of their masculinity and humanity.*

Kesey himself recalls the events that prompted his best-known and sometimes controversial work. In an essay entitled "Who Flew Over What?" and published in *Kesey's Garage Sale* (1973), he writes:

> Finally only the grinning echos remain, the pencilled flesh rearing outta the past in authoritarian attitudes, like guides in a museum tour leading us back to nineteensixty or so . . . and me, a stoodunt, gets asked by my buddy, a sighcologiz, does I wanna go over to the local VA nuthouse, sign up for

Barbara Tepa Lupack, "Hail to the Chief: *One Flew over the Cuckoo's Nest*," in *Insanity as Redemption in Contemporary American Fiction: Inmates Running the Asylum*, Gainesville, FL: University Press of Florida, 1995, pp. 64–98. Copyright © 1995 by the Board of Commissioners of State Institutions of Florida. Reprinted courtesy of the University Press of Florida.

the government experiment, take some of these new mind-altering chemicals?

Does I get paid? I wanna know.

Twenty bucks a session, he says.

All right, I say. Long as it's for the U S of A.

. . . and me, a jock, never even been drunk but that one night in my frat house before my wedding and even then not too drunk—just a token toot for my brothers' benefit—going to the *nut house* to take *dope* under of course official auspices. . .

"See anything yet?" asks the doctor.

"Nope," I tell him, visions swirling indescribable between us.

"How about auditory, any sounds?"

"Not a thing." Just the room full of men outside my door (the experiment being conducted on an actual ward) clamoring their mutual misery, calling with every word and laugh and cough for help, for light, for God at least. . .

Six hours later out of my room on the ward back in the doctor's office he gives me a check for twenty dollars, pulling on a smile like it was a surgical mask, and tells me come back again next Tuesday when "We'll try another one on you." "What was this one?"

"It's called lysergic acid diethylamide twenty-five."

I was there on the next Tuesday, and the next and the next. Six weeks later I'd bought my first ounce of grass. Six months later I had a job at that hospital as a psychiatric aide, and an issue of white uniforms, and a key that opened the doctor's office.

After a few months in his new position, Kesey settled into a midnight-to-eight shift which gave him stretches of five to six hours, five days a week, during which he "had nothing to do but a little mopping and buffing, check the wards every forty-five minutes with a flashlight, be coherent to the night nurse stopping by on her hourly rounds, write my novel, and talk to the sleepless nuts." With access to the various medicines, Kesey would often write under the influence of drugs.

Peyote Inspired Bromden's Character

During one of these sessions, he got the inspiration for Chief Bromden, the novel's narrator. Tom Wolfe, in *The Electric Kool-Aid Acid Test*, reports that "for some reason peyote does this . . . Kesey starts getting eyelid movies of faces . . . from out of nowhere. He knows nothing about Indians and has never met an Indian, but suddenly here is a full-blown Indian—Chief Broom—the solution, the whole mothering key, to the novel."

Peyote was the inspiration for Chief, Kesey claimed, "because it was after choking down eight of the little cactus plants that I wrote the first three pages. These pages remained almost completely unchanged through the numerous rewrites the book went through, and from this first spring I drew all the passion and perception the narrator spoke with during the ten month's writing that followed." Kesey attributed the fact that the narrator was an Indian to the well-known association between peyote and certain tribes of the southwest. "'The drug's reputation is bound to make one think of our red brothers,' was how I used to explain it to admiring fans"—though now even he admits the story seems a bit apocryphal.

However Chief came to be, it is his first-person narration—highly subjective and often hallucinatory—that gives *Cuckoo's Nest* its metaphoric richness, its peculiar horror, and ultimately its emotional force. In fact, to render successfully and credibly Chief's schizophrenic point of view, Kesey felt he needed more than the initial, if fortuitous, hit of peyote and so he precipitated temporary mock-psychotic states in himself through the continued use of psychomimetic [mimicking psychosis] drugs and even arranged to be given electroshock therapy. The writing of the novel "on the ward and on drugs" was, according to him, a way of "double-checking my material so to speak," and the resulting account of Chief's condition, so grimly accurate, is an excellent portrait of contemporary man fragmented, debilitated, and emasculated by institutionalized technology (a familiar theme among contemporary writers, especially [Kurt] Vonnegut). What makes *Cuckoo's Nest* so memorable is the way that the individual ultimately triumphs over the institution's anonymous horrors: the inmates learn to run the asylum and finally, like Bromden, they discover how to escape it completely and make themselves whole and potent again.

The Chief's Identity Is Lost

Few characters in fact or fiction could survive over two hundred electroshock therapy treatments (ESTs), but the hulking six-foot-eight, almost 300-pound Chief is a giant of a man. A former high school athlete and a combat veteran of World War II, he possesses enormous physical strength. In the dehumanized and dehumanizing environment of the Combine and Nurse Ratched's ward, however, he feels small, puny, and incapable of real action. Nicknamed Chief Broom, he is reduced to a topic of ridicule for the Black orderlies and regarded simply as an object, indistinguishable from the broom that he pushes. Virtually his only moving appendage, the broom symbolizes his impotence, both in American society and in the institution that serves as a microcosm of that society. Yet his metamorphosis from a man once so mighty that he speared salmon barehanded to a mere tool for the Nurse's staff has more than a sexual dimension; it also illustrates the central contrast in the book, of machine (or "inside," typified by the wheels and cogs of the Combine, whose agent is the Big Nurse Ratched and whose victims are the emasculated inmates) vs.

nature (or "outside," typified by the world of natural sights and smells away from the Combine, a world that exists for the fog-enshrouded patients only in memory and recollection).

As Barry Leeds demonstrates in his excellent study of Kesey's work, even Chief's legal name, a kind of false identity imposed upon him by others, is a depreciation of his worth. His father, a once shrewd and powerful tribal chief whose Indian name Tee Ah Millatoona meant "The-Pine-That-Stands-Tallest-on-the-Mountain," was so henpecked by the white woman who became his wife (and who represents the pressure brought upon Indians by white American society) that—in a reversal of marital customs in both Indian and white societies—he changed his name and adopted hers. This abandonment of his native heritage, compounded by the subsequent usurping of his land by the government, caused Tee Ah Millatoona to lose his identity entirely. The repercussions of this loss, which Kesey invests with great significance, are felt most strongly by their son, who also bears his mother's name of Bromden and not his father's Indian one. . . .

Bromden responds to the erosion of his identity by pretending to be a deaf mute. Initially unable—and later unwilling—to communicate with others, he progressively withdraws from society. But, as he notes, that society had already withdrawn from him: "it wasn't me that started acting deaf; it was people that first started acting like I was too dumb to hear or see or say anything at all." Even as a young boy he felt his invisibility in a white man's world and learned that Indians are misfits, bereft of any real sense of self. He remembers how, when he was ten, the government agents who came to appropriate his tribe's lands dismissed him as an "overdone little Hiawatha" and then overlooked him completely. Droning on in front of him about the squalor and primitivism of his family's adobe hut, the sole female agent in the group—"an old white-haired woman in an outfit so stiff and heavy it must be armor plate" who bore a striking resemblance in appearance, tone, attitude, and mechanical demeanor to Ratched—didn't bother to listen when he spoke. Moreover, she prevented the other agents from attempting to negotiate with his father, the chief, because direct contact with Mrs. Bromden, a white woman more familiar with government and technology, would make "our job . . . a great deal easier." Other incidents in the community and later in the service (when he watches a buddy at Anzio tied to a tree, screaming for help and water, but is unable to respond for fear "they'd of cut me in half"; or when superiors—"anybody with more stripes" ignored him and treated him as if he were too stupid to respond) cause Bromden to question his own worth, and eventually he assumes the cover of complete silence to avoid such painful engagements altogether. This kind of self-induced mutism, shared by characters as diverse as Oskar Matzerath in [Günter Grass's] *The Tin Drum* (1962), the nameless Boy in [Jerzy Kosinski's] *The Painted Bird* (1965), and the violated heroine, Anna, in [Walker Percy's] *Lancelot* (1977), is, in contemporary literature, an effective symbol for alienation. Within the asylum walls, however, Chief is further alienated; he becomes just one more hopeless case lost in the anonymity of the institution, and no one even tries anymore to communicate with him.

Repeated visits to the asylum's "Shock Shop" have left Bromden in a mental twilight zone that he calls "the fog," a decidedly unnatural element which represents for him the perversion and corruption by Big Nurse and the mechanistic Combine of all that is natural. Serving throughout the novel as a barometer of his emotional and psychological state, the imaginary fog thickens and dissipates according to the fluctuations of his mental and spiritual health. Although the fog exists only in Chief's muddled mind, the "machine" that he thinks produces it has a basis in two very real, very painful experiences: the tranquilizing but brain-benumbing EST treatments ordered by Ratched, and the actual fog machine of

World War II, operated by military intelligence to hide what was occurring on the airfield. "Whenever intelligence figured there might be a bombing attack," recalls Chief, "or if the generals had something secret they wanted to pull—out of sight, hid so good that even the spies on the base couldn't see what went on—they fogged the field." (Ironically, Bromden is correct in suggesting that the real fog is the larger institutional bureaucracy of the military, as evidenced also in [Joseph Heller's] *Catch-22*, [Kurt Vonnegut's] *Slaughterhouse-Five*, and [William Styron's] *Sophie's Choice.*)

Chief believes that the Combine's authority figures have installed a similar machine in the walls of the ward to weaken and control him—an instrument of deception which can distort his thinking and contain him within the artificial order of the institution. Yet after a while, Chief accedes to the fog's hypnotic thickness. "You had a choice," he explains; "you could either strain and look at things that appeared in front of you in the fog, painful as it might be, or you could relax and lose yourself." In his quiet desperation, he opts for the latter.

Chief Rediscovers His Manhood

But Chief's recovery is contingent upon his reentry into the world of the living, particularly the community of nature. For him, though, it is a long journey back: with the exception of the Chronics, he is the patient who is the most far gone and therefore the hardest to reach. Only with the help of Randle Patrick (Mack) McMurphy, the new arrival in the asylum, is Chief able to begin sorting out what is real and what is not. As he learns to distinguish between fact and hallucinatory fantasy, he redevelops some of his manhood and asserts his new strength. Over Ratched's objection, he casts the crucial (but disqualified) vote to watch the World Series on television. Chief's vote not only breaks the 20-20 tie; it makes twenty-one, "a majority," significant here as the legal age of manhood and also the winning hand in blackjack. He joins the other patients on the excursion away from the asylum, a male bonding ritual which builds his confidence and prepares him for his return to the natural world "outside"; and afterwards, at McMurphy's urging (in a special and secret bond between them), lifts the control panel in anticipation of his ultimate escape.

But as the fog diminishes, Chief finds that his new, unobfuscated vision is painful. It hurts, he says, "the way I was hurt by seeing things in the Army, in the war. The way I was hurt by seeing what happened to Papa and the tribe." Without the security of the fog to separate him from his traumatic reality, he becomes more aware of the world and thus more vulnerable to the dangers inherent in it. Yet only by confronting the forces that initially caused him to lose his identity and propelled him into the fog—the petticoat tyranny of his mother, the bitterness of Anzio, the sadness at the loss of Columbia Gorge—can Chief successfully escape it. Bromden starts to use the negative experiences in constructive and instructive ways, to reorganize the sources of his own pain and paralysis so that each time he recalls key moments in his past, he retrieves a part of himself and becomes more conscious. Every recollection of a painful memory marks a return to health, and only out of these fragments can he become whole again.

The further Chief moves out of the fog, the more the nature of his narrative changes. No longer tentative and fantasylike, his story becomes stronger, more lyrical. The paranoiac hallucinations about the cogs of the Combine machine that pervade the early parts of the novel give way to a clarity, even a poetry. Perhaps the best example of the change is in Chief's recounting of an earlier conversation with McMurphy. Heading back to the ward after the fishing trip, they drove through the town in which McMurphy had lived as a boy. The sight of a rag hanging from a tree branch reminded Mack of his first sexual experience, which had occurred when he was ten and which established his reputation as a "dedicated lover." The memory of that experience prompted Mack to share the details with Chief, who was not at all surprised to learn that his new friend's sense of identity and mission had always been secure; after all, even in the asylum Mack maintained a strong sense of his individuality. On admission, he corrects Ratched's mispronunciation of his name and warns her never to call him "Mr. McMurry" again. Chief, on the other hand, has lost his identity and prefers the anonymity that his muteness and the Combine's fog provide. Yet his recollection and appreciation of Mack's story (a contemporary parallel to the naming scenes in heroic epics) demonstrates his growing recognition that identity is destiny; it is evident that Chief is beginning very consciously to prepare himself for the power that McMurphy will transfer to him. "I noticed vaguely that I was getting so's I could see some good in the life around me. McMurphy was teaching me. I was feeling better than I'd remembered feeling since I was a kid, when everything was good and the land was still singing kid's poetry to me." . . .

Chief as Moral Voice

Because Chief has been on the ward longer than any of the other inmates—longer than anyone else, except Big Nurse—he is familiar with all of Ratched's tactics as well as the adverse effects of her destructive therapies. He therefore serves not only as narrator of *One Flew Over the Cuckoo's Nest* but as its central intelligence, who provides a kind of implicit moral commentary on the happenings on the ward. Like Nick Carraway in [F. Scott Fitzgerald's] *The Great Gatsby*, Ishmael in [Herman Melville's] *Moby-Dick*, and Stingo in [William Styron's] *Sophie's Choice*, he not only records the events but also interprets them. And like the narrator of "A Rose for Emily," whose sympathy for the heroine allows him to see her as an icon and a town monument and not as a pathological eccentric, his affectionate vision of McMurphy as deliverer rather than as profiteer defines the novel.

Although years of conditioning have inured Chief to the deadly monotony of the asylum and taught him that "Whoever comes in the door is usually somebody disappointing," McMurphy manages to surprise him. He doesn't simply slide along the wall, as new admissions generally do; instead he explodes on the scene, like the bombs of which Scanlon dreams. On the ward where all men are made to feel small, even McMurphy's voice "sounds big. . . . He talks a little the way Papa used to, voice loud and full of hell." When McMurphy, only minutes after his arrival, dismisses the orderlies who try to steer him to the shower and plants himself firmly in the day room, thumbs in his pockets, boots wide apart like some mythic cartoon character or cocky Western hero, Chief is convinced he is some magical giant fallen from the skies. And when McMurphy laughs out loud at the absurdity of the situation on the ward, Chief immediately recognizes that "this sounds real . . . it's the first laugh I've heard in years." It is so loud and so real that it registers on the machinery of the institution: "Dials twitch in the control panel at the sound of it." The unfamiliar sound stuns everyone; they look spooked and uneasy, "the way kids look in a schoolroom when one ornery kid is raising too much hell with the teacher out of the room and they're all scared the teacher might pop back in and take it into her head to make them all stay after." Even the Acute inmates sense that this red-headed Irish brawler is "different from anybody been coming on this ward for the past ten years, different from anybody they ever met outside."

McMurphy *is* different: his resonant voice and hearty laugh pierce the silent void and assail the asylum's order. Yet his very disruption of the mechanical routine is a restoration of normalcy. Like the Grail Knight who returns life to the wasteland, McMurphy's eccentric behavior generates some passion in an otherwise passionless environment. Unwilling merely to bear passive witness to the other inmates' lethargy, he fills the sterile ward with sounds long unheard—ribald jokes and songs,

Danny DeVito (as Martini) and others in a scene from the 1975 film adaptation of Ken Kesey's One Flew over the Cuckoo's Nest. *United Artists/Fantasy Films/The Kobal Collection/The Picture Desk, Inc.*

which echo in the halls and challenge the Combine's authority as they revive the patients' saltpetered [made impotent] spirits. His laughter is especially welcome because it is unlike the derisive and belittling noises the inmates are used to: the snickering orderlies, "mumbling . . . and humming hate and death and other hospital secrets"; the falsity of "Public Relation," leading his tours through "mother" Ratched's model ward; the tight-lipped pleasantries of the hypocritical Big Nurse and her surrogates. . . .

McMurphy Helps Chief Regain Manhood

Unused as they are to humor, the men don't laugh easily at first. The institution itself prohibits it; Chief says "the air is pressed in by the walls, too tight for laughing. There's something strange about a place where the men won't let themselves loose and laugh." Billy "opens his mouth but can't say a thing," and only after McMurphy ribs him about his sexual prowess (and physically gooses him in the process) does he finally blush and grin a little. Harding tries to laugh but makes merely a "mousy little squeak." And Chief doesn't speak or laugh at all. When he finally utters his first words and attempts to laugh along with McMurphy, "it was a squawking sound, like a pullet trying to crow. It sounded more like crying than laughing." Even for a performer as seasoned as McMurphy, the inmates prove to be a tough audience. He has to manipulate them, the way a carny operator—an image Kesey uses several times to describe McMurphy—works his crowd. "He's being the clown," says Chief, "working at getting some of the guys to laugh. It bothers him that the best they can do is grin weakly and snigger sometimes."

McMurphy, though, persists. "He knows you have to laugh at the things that hurt you just to keep yourself in balance, just to keep the world from running you plumb crazy," observes Chief. "He knows there's a painful side . . . but he won't let the pain blot out the humor no more'n he'll let the humor blot out the pain." And he realizes that once the men are able to laugh at themselves, they will be less likely to be hurt by the vitriolic remarks of Ratched and her staff.

In addition to giving them the gift of healing laughter, McMurphy touches the patients with a friendly hand that helps them to regain their potency. As soon as he is admitted, he makes a point of shaking hands with everyone. The human touching contrasts with the cold and sterile treatment they receive from Big Nurse; his is a warm, natural, spontaneous gesture, unlike her mechanical actions. Consequently McMurphy's big hand, symbolizing masculinity and power, becomes the answer to Ratched's momism and represents his power to save the inmates from the deadly and emasculating monotony of her ward. . . .

Having shown them that they can function as individuals within the asylum walls, McMurphy decides to prove to the inmates, most of whom are voluntary admissions, that they can manage outside the institution as well. With the help of his "aunt" Candy, a woman far sweeter in every regard than "mother" Ratched, he arranges a fishing excursion and cons Dr. Spivey into accompanying the group and legitimizing the experience for them. (The doctor, who feels overwhelmed by Ratched, is in almost as much need of a cure as the inmates are.) When they stop at a filling station, however, the attendant intimidates the doctor by trying to foist on him various needless items such as oil filters and sunglasses before he will pump their gas. McMurphy won't abide the cheap hustle: he stands up to the attendant—one con man to another—and literally puts his hands in the man's face and holds them there "a long time, waiting to see if the guy had anything else to say." The man immediately backs down; Mack's bravado restores the tenor of the trip and leaves the whole group feeling as "cocky as fighting roosters."

At the dock, when they encounter another obstacle, McMurphy once again saves the day by commandeering a fishing boat and launching the expedition. But as the inmates start landing fish and calling for his assistance, he stands aside, refusing to help them out. Even after Candy's breast is bloodied by the reeling line and Chief's thumb is cut and everyone is unnerved and exhausted by the exertion of catching a big fish, he keeps watching and laughing but remains conspicuously detached. His uncharacteristic passivity is not a sign of callousness or indifference; nor is it the result of increasing physical weakness. Rather, it is a demonstration of real caring. McMurphy knows that mere example is not enough of an answer to the men's problems: he must empower them to act on their own behalf. By forcing them to use their own hands, to rely on their own resources and to feel responsible for each other, he allows them to reclaim their identity as independent functioning persons. Soon they are able to laugh loudly "at their own selves as well as at the rest of us" and when they dock, even the locals who had belittled them must acknowledge their skill in capturing the biggest fish anyone has ever seen.

The fishing trip, which serves as a kind of Pentecost for all aboard, not only shows the men that the way out of the institution is to return to the natural values of the world "outside"; it also encourages them to grow both individually and collectively. Their camaraderie sustains them back on the ward, where they celebrate their victory by standing up to Ratched. Ultimately, only their collective force defeats her forceful collective, which has—until late—steadily eroded their confidence and self-worth.

From the beginning, no one benefits more from Mack's friendly hand than Bromden. Whereas others have come to take Chief's hulking silence for granted, McMurphy pays attention to him and manages to bring him back from his self-imposed silence by offering him a stick of Juicy Fruit. (The black orderly had earlier removed Chief's stash of used gum from under his bed. Feigning muteness, Chief could not object; and being indigent, unlike most of the other inmates, he had no money to buy new gum.) Thus McMurphy's act of friendship—but even more of understanding—prompts Chief to utter "thank you," the first words he has spoken since coming to the asylum soon after the war. When McMurphy then unties Bromden's bed sheets and promises to make him big again, he helps to eliminate other restrictions that have bound Chief and kept him feeling small. The restoration of a part of Bromden's psychological manhood long repressed has an obvious sexual dimension as well; just by talking about the spectacular results Chief will see from Mack's special "body-building course," he helps Chief to experience his first erection in years. ("Look there, Chief. Haw. What'd I tell ya? You growed a half a foot already.") And by signing Chief up for the fishing excursion and paying for his share, McMurphy gives him the courage he needs to defy the aides for the first time and to stand up for himself as a man. The next morning, "When they stuck a broom out for me to do their work up the hall," Chief says, "I turned around and walked back to the dorm, telling myself, The hell with that. A man goin' fishing with two whores from Portland don't have to take that crap." His potency regained, Chief does not need the broom's dead wood to define him ever again.

Chief reciprocates when McMurphy's self-sacrifice renders him incapable of further struggle. Effectively reversing their roles, Chief assumes McMurphy's power and responsibility. To save Mack, now a symbolically castrated and literally lobotomized shell of a man, from further abuse, Chief smothers him. "I was only sure of one thing: he wouldn't have left something like that sit there in the day room with his name tacked on it for twenty or thirty years so the Big Nurse could use it as an example of what can happen if you buck the system. I was sure of that." But even in his vegetal state McMurphy retains a tough grip on life. To suffocate him, Chief must climb up on his bed in an almost sexual posture ([critic] Leslie Fiedler calls it "a caricature of the act of love"); he recalls lying "full length on top of [McMurphy]" and "scissor[ing] the kicking legs with mine while I mashed the pillow into the face. I lay there on top of the body for what seemed days. Until the thrashing stopped. Until it was still a while and had shuddered once and was still again. Then I rolled off." . . .

In the tub room, Chief lifts the control panel, which represents the monolithic weight of the Combine, a machinery that seems to be invulnerable to the efforts of any single man to move it; he heaves it through the screen and the window— the same escape route McMurphy had planned to use for his breakout—with a ripping crash. "Like a bright cold water baptizing the sleeping earth," the glass shatters and a reborn Chief vaults to freedom, leaving behind him forever the fog and the Combine and Big Nurse's frozen smile. He runs toward the highway and heads west, to the Columbia Gorge and his tribal land, to reestablish his sense of self, because he has "been away a long time." With his powerful hands, Mack shook the asylum; with his even stronger hands, Chief all but destroys it and everything for which it stands. . . .

Patients Regain Sanity and Humanity

As the many symbols and images indicate, the central theme of *One Flew Over the Cuckoo's Nest* is the restoration of the inmates' individual and collective potency. But potency, for Kesey, is much more than mere sexuality: it is the strong assertion of identity and the firm belief in the strength of the individual as sufficient to challenge mindless regimen. McMurphy saves the men from being swallowed up in the technological horror and anonymity of the institution by making them aware of their own manhood, in the sense of both their masculinity and their humanity. To read the novel literally as a diatribe against women and a celebration of white male chauvinism, as some commentators and critics have, is to neglect this second dimension; such a narrow reading also overlooks the fact that Kesey is questioning, not describing or applauding, such societal stereotypes. . . .

The majority of readers of *One Flew Over the Cuckoo's Nest* have not missed the comedy of it, as evidenced by the novel's tremendous and enduring success. First made popular by a generation that saw in McMurphy's rebellion against the Big Nurse and Chief's escape from the ward an allegory for the struggle of the Vietnam years, the novel continues to appeal to a new generation of readers, equally frustrated by institutions that have abused their authority and betrayed those whom they were designed to protect. As symbols of resistance to a repressive system, the mad heroes McMurphy and Bromden merely corroborate what another nonconformist, [poet] Emily Dickinson, wrote more than a century ago: "Much Madness is Divinest Sense." It is through their almost divine madness that the real insanity of the asylum—and of contemporary society—is exposed.

Kesey Creates an Oedipal Triangle in *Cuckoo's Nest*

Ruth Sullivan

Ruth Sullivan was an English professor at Northeastern University who also wrote for such journals as Studies in Romanticism *and* Studies in American Fiction.

In the following essay, Sullivan finds it ironic that Ken Kesey satirizes psychological theories and psychiatrists in One Flew over the Cuckoo's Nest *at the same time that he portrays a twist on the classic Freudian Oedipal triangle in the book. In Sigmund Freud's classic theory of psychological development a child goes through three phases: 1) the oral phase (based on nursing at the breast), in which one learns or is denied emotional comfort and security; 2) the anal phase (based on toilet training), in which one learns or rejects control; and 3) the phallic phase (based on sexuality), which is characterized by the formation and resolution (or not) of the Oedipus Complex (referring to the ancient Greek character who unwittingly kills his father and marries his mother), in which the child wants to bond with the mother and eliminate the father who is the child's rival for the mother's attention and affection. Sullivan also mentions Freud's theory of the structure of the psyche, which consists of the id (seat of unconscious desires and pleasure-seeking), the ego (the conscious sense of self), and the superego (the learned complex of rules, obedience, and conscience).*

Sullivan suggests that Big Nurse is the mother figure, McMurphy the father figure, and the rest of the inmates are the sons. The maternal force is controlling and mechanical; the paternal force is one of freedom and nature. But in this Oedipal triangle, the issue confronting them is not sex, but power.

Ruth Sullivan, "Big Mama, Big Papa, and Little Sons in Ken Kesey's *One Flew over the Cuckoo's Nest*," *Literature and Psychology*, vol. 25, no. 1, 1975, pp. 34–44. Copyright © Editor 1975. Reproduced by permission of *Literature & Pyschology: A Psychoanalytic and Cultural Criticism*.

Sigmund Freud is something less than a culture hero in Ken Kessey's *One Flew Over the Cuckoo's Nest*. What else but destructive can one call a psychoanalytically informed therapy that brands McMurphy's rebellion against the institution's ego-murder as "schizophrenic reaction," his love of "poozle" and pretty girls as "Latent Homosexual with Reaction Formation" or, with emphasis, "Negative Oedipal"? Kesey portrays the psychiatrists and residents as patsies of Big Nurse Ratched, and portrays her as a power-maniac running a small machine within that big machine, Society (the "Combine"). Psychoanalytic therapy in this novel dehumanizes because it serves not people but technology.

Ratched Emasculates Patients

Ironic then, is the fact that while the novel disparages psychoanalytic therapy, it compliments psychoanalytic theory in that Kesey structures human relationships in *Cuckoo's Nest* after his own understanding of Freud's delineation of the Oedipus complex. That is, Kesey presents the typical oedipal triangle of mother, father, and sons in Nurse Ratched, Randle McMurphy, and Chief Bromden plus the other inmates of the asylum. And he dramatizes some typical oedipal conflicts: the sons witness encounters, often explicitly sexual, between the father and mother figures, and the crucial emotional issue for the sons is how to define their manliness in relation to the mother figure and with the help of and ability to identify with the father.

That Kesey intends Nurse Ratched to play Big Mama not only to Chief Bromden but also to the other characters is evident by the many references to her often perverted maternal qualities. To Public Relations she is "just like a mother." He believes in "that tender little mother crap" as McMurphy puts it, but the big Irishman and soon the other inmates see through "that smiling flour-faced old mother" with her "big, womanly breast." Chief Bromden observes Big Nurse draw

Billy's "cheek to her starched breast, stroking his shoulder. . . ." Meanwhile, "she continued to glare at us as she spoke. It was strange to hear that voice, soft and soothing and warm as a pillow, coming out of a face hard as porcelain." "We are victims of a matriarchy here, my friend," Harding says to McMurphy. "Man has but *one* truly effective weapon against that juggernaut of modern matriarchy," rape, and McMurphy is elected to do it.

Why rape? Because Kesey's Big Mama is a "ball-cutter," in McMurphy's language, and the men must protect themselves. Harding, too, understands that one of Big Nurse's most effective methods of control is to render the men impotent: Dr. Spivey by subtle insinuations about his need for drugs and by depriving him of real authority; Billy Bibbit, by threatening to tell his mother about his night with the prostitute; and the young residents by making them fear her judgment on their professional performance. "There's not a man here that isn't afraid he is losing or has already lost his whambam," says Harding. "We comical little creatures can't even achieve masculinity in the rabbit world, that's how weak and inadequate we are. Hee. We are the *rabbits* one might say, of the rabbit world!" Harding even sees that to the Nurse, lobotomies are symbolic castrations: "Yes; chopping away the brain. Frontal-lobe castration. I guess if she can't cut below the belt she'll do it above the eyes."

Big Nurse should be keeping those in her care warm and fed and healthy; she should be loving but is instead denying, destructive, and terrifying. Big Daddy, in Randle McMurphy's Big Daddyhood, is only a little less obvious than Nurse Ratched's warped maternity. "Like the logger, . . . the swaggering gambler . . . the cowboy out of the TV set . . .", Randle McMurphy booms upon the scene, his heels striking fire out of the tiles, his huge seamed hand extended to lift the inmates out of fear and into freedom. He renews their almost lost sense of manliness by denying Harding's description of them as "rabbits *sans* whambam," by having them deep-sea fish, gamble, and party it up with pretty little whores, by encouraging the men (himself as an example) to flirt with the nurses, by spinning virility fantasies, and by introducing Billy to women. He teaches them to laugh and to revolt against Ratched's tyranny, and he often protects them while they are growing. . . .

At Issue Is Power, Not Sex

Kesey sketches in the oedipal triangle, then, in dramatizing an intense emotional relationship among father, mother, and son figures and by having the father teach the sons what it means to be a man. He teaches them about self-assertion, aggression, fun, and sex—the latter sometimes in relationship to Big Nurse. After all, the inmates expect McMurphy to make Ratched into a woman by performing some sexual act with her and McMurphy eventually does that. Meanwhile, he acts sexually toward her by making teasing remarks about her big breasts.

But Kesey gives the reader his own unique version of the oedipal struggle. What the sons witness in the interaction between Big Nurse and Randle McMurphy is pseudosex. The most urgent emotional issue between them is really power. McMurphy will strip Big Nurse, but he will do so in vengeful destruction of her power. When he teases her about her womanly body suppressed by the starched uniform, his motive is to humiliate her. When he takes up the inmates' challenge to best Big Nurse he says:

> I've never seen a woman I thought was more than me, I don't care whether I can get it up for her or not. . . . So I'm saying five bucks to each of you that wants it I can't put a betsy bug up that nurse's butt within a week. . . . Just that. A bee in her butt, a burr in her bloomers. Get her goat.

The imagery here is not genital but anal. He wants to be free of her control, wants to be in control himself, and wants the inmates to gain self-control and control over Big Nurse. So, the central symbolic act in the novel and the unseating and destruction of the control panel. Big Nurse herself is a caricature of the anal personality, a typical obsessive-compulsive creature with those typical needs for order, cleanliness, and power, with the tendency to treat people like objects, the inability to relax and to relate to others with tolerance for their frailties. Chief Bromden associates her with machinery, whiteness, frost, starch, cleanliness, rules, time, manipulation, and the Combine. She does try to castrate her sons, but it is in the interest of power. She denies them warmth, autonomy, and manhood in order to keep her own world intact. Her biggest fear, and the sign of her defeat, is loss of control.

It seems, then, that in Kesey's version of the oedipal struggle, the sons learn that mature women are dangerous because they want to emasculate (i.e., to control so as to incapacitate) their men. Almost every woman who stands in an explicitly sexual relationship to men in the novel poses a threat to her man's virility. Billy Bibbit's mother and the wives of Harding and Ruckly . . . are the most blatant examples. . . .

Kesey's oedipal triangle . . . is not casebook pure. It bears the stamp of the preceding emotional phase [in Freud's theory], the anal, in which the crucial issues are control over one's own body and the environment, rebellion and submission, autonomy and shame. Such a pattern works itself out in the novel thus: the oedipal elements revolve around the wish of the sons to love and be loved by adult women and by the women originally closest to them, mother and Big Nurse. They turn to the father, McMurphy, as role model; he teaches them by anecdote and example how to be men. The anal elements color this pattern because the sons are frustrated in their desires toward a woman as threatening as Big Nurse. They want to be men, but she wants them to be automatons; they want to love, but she wants to control. Because Big Nurse manages every aspect of their lives—their bodies, activities, shelter—she deprives them of autonomy. Oedipal elements mixed with anal reappear when McMurphy both "feminizes" Big Nurse, in his symbolic rape that exposes her breasts, and dethrones her, breaks her control.

Further, the novel displays emotional conflicts even more primitive than these, for if the men fear woman because she can emasculate her man (a phallic issue) or because she can control him (an anal issue), they also fear her because she withholds emotional warmth and physical care (oral issues). A deep disappointment that the novel expresses concerning women is not only their failure to be equal and generous partners to men, or even their unwillingness to submit to men in a battle of the sexes, but their failure to play a warmly maternal role, or, when actually assuming that role, their failure to play it effectively.

Though Nurse Ratched is an obvious example of this, almost all other women in the novel are, too. . . .

It is impossible to know accurately how much of Kesey's delineation of the Oedipus complex is deliberate and how much is inevitable revelation of his own complexes. He clearly labels his Big Mama, Big Daddy, and little sons; but when he involves them in a power struggle and in a search for a generous, caretaking mother, likely his emotional constellations are no longer consciously created. But our subject is not biography; it is interpretation of one work of art. Hence we might ask how Kesey's oral, anal, and oedipal patterns, deliberate and not, influence a reader's emotional response and interpretation of themes. . . .

Bromden Unlikely to Recover

In oedipal terms, the novel promises that the matriarchy cannot be defeated. To do battle with it means the castration of the father and most of the sons—indeed, all of the sons, for the rehabilitation of Chief Bromden is fairy tale, not reality. He has been on the ward nearly twenty years; he has had over two hundred shock treatments; and he is, by the revelations of his own speech, a paranoid schizophrenic. A man so deeply scarred is unlikely to recover so completely in a few months, no matter how brilliant his model and nurturer is.

This anxiety-filled fantasy of mechanical, destructive motherhood cannot account for the enthusiasm of Kesey's readers any more than can the genius of the style or plotting. The latter two are significant, of course, but for reasons beyond the aesthetic or intellectual pleasures they afford. The novel must also create other, more satisfying fantasies, as well as a defense against its nuclear fantasy that is effective enough to make a reader, especially a young one, feel not only reassured but triumphant.

One of the appeals of the novel is the opportunity it affords its readers to feel unjustly persecuted and to revel in self-pity: "Poor little me. See how helpless and good I am; yet They hurt me." Because persecution of those undeserving sets the tone for *One Flew Over the Cuckoo's Nest*, a reader can scarcely escape the novel's stimulation of these unconscious feelings in himself. Everyone has in his early life experienced the apparent omnipotence and omniscience of adults who, on occasion, must frustrate the demands of their infants and must therefore seem unjust, even cruel. But such experiences are usually painful. Why should their arousal in *Cuckoo's Nest* prove delightful? Because, first, the novel is convincing about the power of the Combine and its agent, Nurse Ratched. Americans particularly have reason to feel oppressed by Big Government, Big Business, and Big Industry and to be convinced that the individual alone can do little to influence them to his benefit or to prevent their harming him. Chief Bromden is paranoic, but not everything in his vision is false: "You think the guy telling this is ranting and raving my *God*; you think this is too horrible to have really happened, this is too awful to be the truth!. . . But it's the truth even if it didn't happen." The novel offers its readers a sympathetic forum, a

justification for feeling oppressed, even congratulations for being so sensitive as to have those feelings. Kesey's novel says, in
effect, that someone understands.

A second reason for the pleasure-in-persecution feelings
evoked in the reader's unconscious by *Cuckoo's Nest* is this:
"poor little me" fantasies are pleasurable if one knows that
one's audience is kindly and even effective against the alleged
or actual abuse. The antiestablishment, antityranny tone of
the novel answers these needs: so does the person of McMurphy because he functions the way a powerful father figure
might against a cruel mother. The plaint of injustice is largely
carried by the helpless inmates; their target is Big Nurse and
the Combine; their forum and protection is McMurphy. Finally, one might speculate that being unjustly persecuted is
pleasant if it arouses one's masochism and if it provides a
sense of moral superiority: "You may be bigger than I am but
I am superior to you in other, especially moral, ways." *Cuckoo's
Nest* dramatically demonstrates the righteousness and good-
ness of the inmates over Big Nurse, her cohorts, and the Combine. And of course she is overthrown. Injustice may live, but
in *Cuckoo's Nest* it does not thrive.

The novel also richly gratifies latent or conscious hostile
impulses against authority. Obviously, the novel delights in
jibes and pain inflicted upon Nurse Ratched. (An audience
applauds whenever Big Nurse is bested in the play; it even
hisses and boos when the actress who plays her takes her
bow.) But the book allows expression of hostile impulses toward loved authorities as well, for the inmates not only care
about McMurphy, they also resent him. Big Nurse succeeds in
turning most of them against him for a while when she hints
that he exploits them. Billy Bibbit turns against him when
caught in his sexual misdemeanor. They all use him to fight
their battles, egg him on to engage Big Nurse when they, but
not McMurphy, know that he can be punished in the "Brain
Murdering" room. Most significantly, they kill him. They are

responsible for his lobotomy: "We couldn't stop him [from attacking Big Nurse] because we were the ones making him do it. It wasn't the Nurse that was forcing him, it was our need that was making him push himself slowly up . . .".

Chief Bromden performs an actual killing. Manifestly, the deed is euthanasia; symbolically, it is an enacted crucifixion; thematically, it is evidence that the son has grown up and surpassed his father even while loving him; and latently, the killing expresses the ancient hostility of the son to even a loving father.

Exploring Individual Freedom

To permission for indulgence in self-pity and attacks on loved and hated authority figures, the novel adds permission to gratify dependency wishes. A dominant theme of *One Flew Over the Cuckoo's Nest* concerns the nature of individual freedom—political, social, and psychological. It asserts that in the psychological realm, certain kinds of dependence are healthy: the dependence of a child upon good parents, of a patient upon effective nurses and doctors, and of weak adults upon nurturing strong ones. But this dependent condition is healthy only if it fosters eventual independence. Big Nurse destroys because she must control; hence she blocks the autonomy of her patients, whereas McMurphy nurtures because, while he protects, he also encourages the inmates to use their own resources in order to meet the world. This theme, readily apparent to a reader's intelligence, disguises the abundant latent gratification the novel offers one's often unacknowledged pleasure in dependency upon an omnipotent figure. Throughout the novel, with a few exceptions, McMurphy acts on behalf of the patients, acts so magnificently that a reader laughs. "We ain't ordinary nuts; we're every bloody one of us hot off the criminal-insane ward, on our way to San Quentin where they got better facilities to handle us"; so McMurphy informs the gas station attendants who would bully the inmates. Here the weak overpower the strong the way children overpower giants in fairy tales. The inmates overpower Big Nurse when Mc-Murphy, a sort of kindly helper figure also common in fairy tales, shows them how; and they overpower her, in part gayly and jokingly, in part grimly. The childlike fun of the novel, the use of ridicule as a weapon against oppression, and the demonstration on the part of McMurphy that he is a bigger, better person than Big Bad Nurse all contribute to a reader's readiness to accept the novel's tacit invitation: allow yourself to depend upon the good, omnipotent father; he will help you conquer the wicked stepmother.

Cuckoo's Nest is gratifying especially to the young, then, because while it creates an anxiety-ridden fantasy about a destructive mother (and social order), it also creates a powerful, caring father to allay anxiety. In addition, it grants indulgence in certain unconscious needs and wishes to be dependent, to feel unjustly treated (masochistic and moral-righteousness pleasures), and to attack and defeat ambivalently held authority figures (even McMurphy is killed).

To unearth unconscious fantasies as a way of understanding why *One Flew Over the Cuckoo's Nest* is emotionally satisfying is not to dismiss the power or validity of themes one understands intellectually. Indeed, unconscious fantasies isolated from theme in a piece of fiction sound grotesque, perhaps meaningless. In *Cuckoo's Nest* as in all fiction, theme not only gives meaning to unconscious fantasy but also functions as a kind of defense. For instance *Cuckoo's Nest* is usually read as an indictment of our technological society, which, by standardization and forced conformity, murders human brains, even as the shock shop murders the inmates' minds. Psychotherapy is dangerous, this novel alleges, because it has become mechanized, a tool for social control wielded by the Combine. But the novel also affirms that man's drive for independence is so strong that no matter how overwhelming the obstacles, he will break free; it suggests, as well, that perhaps nature will once more nurture man where technology now destroys him.

Kesey's antitechnology, pronature theme is fittingly supported by his deliberate, use of an oedipal triangle marked by a man-woman power struggle, a triangle in which mother acts like a machine against, rather than for, her children, while father tries valiantly to restore them to their own natures and to freedom. The unconscious needs the novel stimulates in its readers also re-enforce the theme. For instance, though men yearn to be free, they also fear autonomy and wish to be dependent. Chief Bromden sits in the cuckoo's nest because he has not the courage to face the world. No more do those voluntarily committed—Billy Bibbit and Harding, say, who admit their fear of leaving the restitution.

Responsible for Their Own Fates

Now *Cuckoo's Nest* has another theme that seems to counterpoint its blatant Darwinian survival-of-the-fittest message. The strong do indeed aggress against the weak; and though a few escape the trap, most are caught and destroyed. But the Combine is only the ostensible enemy; the real one lurks in men's own minds. Just as in a paranoid fantasy the external persecutors are projections of the sufferer's self-hatred, so is the Combine a projection of the destructive power-drive in men—especially in weak, ineffectual men. While *Cuckoo's Nest* does show how the strong oppress the weak, it also shows how the weak can destroy the strong. Chief Bromden understands this at the end of the novel, for he knows that McMurphy attacks Nurse Ratched because the inmates compel him to. Harding understood this earlier. In explaining why he must be institutionalized, he at first blames society:

> It wasn't the practices, I don't think, it was the feeling that the great, deadly, pointing forefinger of society was pointing

at me—and the great voice of millions chanting, "Shame. Shame. Shame." It's society's way of dealing with someone different.

But McMurphy counters that he, too, is different, yet he was not seriously affected. Harding answers:

> "I wasn't giving my reason as the sole reason. Though I used to think at one time, a few years ago . . . that society's chastising was the sole force that drove one along the road to crazy [sic] . . . you've caused me to reappraise my theory. There's something else that drives people, strong people like you, my friend, down that road. . . . It is us!" Harding swept his hand about him in a soft white circle and repeated, "Us."

The theme of *Cuckoo's Nest* is not merely the assertion that society will get you. It also realistically affirms that if society gets you, it is because you have complied in both your own and others' destruction. The weak are tyrants, too, subtle and dangerous because they can wake in the strong a sympathetic identification and perhaps guilt: "Why should I have so much when they have so little? Then, maybe I am in some way responsible for their fate." Like the inmates of the asylum, the weak can unintentionally exploit and cannibalize their benefactors, driving them to ruin. . . .

Kesey does not mislead his readers. For those who choose to hear, he says that while the social order is indeed a mighty, complex organism difficult to understand and more difficult to influence or change, nevertheless men are responsible for their own fates. One must be strong to survive, even stronger to prevail, but if such a man is inspirited with that most valued of American qualities—the drive for independence and freedom—he can make it.

Kesey's novel is a kind of phenomenon, though, for the skillful way in which he manages to be hard-headedly realistic (hence to appeal to the ego), as well as indulgent of so many and such powerful unconscious, even infantile drives (the novel richly gratifies the id) and respectful of certain ethical considerations: the evil are punished, but so are those who inflict punishment; crime does not pay (the superego is appeased). The fact that the theme can be doubly perceived—technology is responsible for man's destruction and men are responsible for their own—both stimulates and manages the anxiety-ridden nuclear fantasy. On the one hand, a reader can fully respond to his own regressive fantasies, and on the other, he is encouraged to pull out of them and cope with external reality. Kesey's use of the oedipal constellation to pattern human relationships in *Cuckoo's Nest* functions in much the same way. The content of the novel damns psychoanalytically informed psychotherapy in such a way as to cater to fantasies of persecution and helplessness; meanwhile, the novel's artistic design uses psychoanalytic theory to reassure the reader (as all skillful handling of artistic form and style does) that nevertheless everything is safe. It is as though Kesey says: "I, the artist, can handle this material, dangerous though it may be. See, I make it part of the solid structure of this novel. You need not be afraid while I am in control." Mama may be dangerous, but Big Daddy is here to protect his children.

Mixed Ethnicity and Gender Issues Present Challenges to Manhood

Robert P. Waxler

Robert P. Waxler teaches in the Department of English at the University of Massachusetts–Dartmouth.

While numerous critics have written about the theme of matriarchy in One Flew over the Cuckoo's Nest, *Waxler suggests in the following selection that few have focused on the equally important issue of ethnicity. He contends that the fact that Chief Bromden has a white mother who has dominated his Native American father is at the root of his problems with his identity and is central to the theme of the novel. According to Waxler, Ken Kesey raises a complex issue—how does a minority male with a dominant white mother achieve manhood in contemporary American society?* Cuckoo's Nest *does not offer a solution, but it does address this important issue.*

Ken Kesey's novel *One Flew Over the Cuckoo's Nest* challenges us with the issue of mixed heritage through Chief Bromden's half-breed status. In this we confront the most significant and unsettling conflict of the text. Although few critics have focused on the issue it is complex enough to have been a part of American fiction throughout the twentieth century. Like [William] Faulkner, Kesey sets his character on a symbolic search for the Father: that is, the spark of manhood within himself that flares at the traditional gender definition. The search is complicated, however, by the father's minority status which gives the mother social supremacy. Moreover, Ke-

Robert P. Waxler, "The Mixed Heritage of the Chief: Revisiting the Problem of Manhood in *One Flew over the Cuckoo's Nest*," *Journal of Popular Culture*, vol. 29, no. 3, Winter 1995, pp. 225–235. Copyright © 1995 Basil Blackwell Ltd. Reproduced by permission of Blackwell Publishers.

sey further hinders the search by making the dominant system throughout the story a demanding and outwardly oppressive matriarchy. The combined elements of gender and mixed heritage form the point, I believe, that makes the novel problematic, not only for the reader, but for Kesey himself.

Bromden's Status Is Central

In an important sense, the family is always the matrix for social and individual identity. We are our family. And in such a context, we need to ask how Chief Bromden can possibly gain back his manhood, in a sense rediscover "the name of the father," when he is rooted in a family which has denied that name, privileging instead the name of his white mother (Bromden). Chief Bromden's problem, in this sense, is the difficulty he faces in attempting to recover the roots of his Native American identity, the identity of his father, that male Indian identity buried deep along the Columbia River in the Dalles.

What the critics seem to have avoided when discussing *One Flew Over The Cuckoo's Nest* is that Bromden's "mixed heritage" is at the root of the Chief's problem of identity, accounting, to a large extent, for his schizophrenic narrative. More specifically, the Chief's family history puts him in the precarious position of a son who believes that his roots can only be discovered through his father, a man with an ethnic minority status. The Chief is a son, in other words, attempting to achieve manhood in a world dominated by women in general (one version of the classic story of the American boy), but specifically by a white mother. As Terence Martin has put it: "The female reduced the male—the white reduced the Indian. The Chief has only to think of his parents to know the legacy of his people." The Chief, that Vanishing American as Kesey calls him, must rediscover not only his legacy as a Native American, but the very roots of his manhood by thinking back through his father, that is through the place of the father, the original territory of the Native American man now overrun by whites. That act of white imperialism in terms of the novel is represented in the first instance by his mother. In this context, we can assume that the Chief's problems would be very different if his mother had been an American Indian.

In a sense, Kesey has given us an Oedipal story with a twist rarely explored by white American novelists, especially before the early 1960s when *Cuckoo's Nest* was written. In the simplest Freudian version of the Oedipal story, if the son is to achieve manhood, he must symbolically kill the father and marry the mother. But what if the father, a member of an ethnic minority, has been marginalized by the mother, a member of the dominant culture? How then does the son recover the authority and power of the father? And how does the son rejuvenate desire for the mother, especially when that mother, in the mind of the son, has become an abstraction, a repressive symbol of the majority culture? These are questions that critics rarely discuss when talking about *Cuckoo's Nest*, yet they are questions central to a full understanding of the novel. They raise issues that help to illuminate the relationship between the racial and sexual identity of the Chief and his narrative perceptions. They help the reader to understand the Chief as an embattled self and as a Vanishing American male.

When the Chief first introduces Big Nurse to the reader, for example, she is carrying her woven wicker bag made by Indians but used by her to carry the tools that she manipulates to maintain her dehumanized control over the ward. Like the Chief's mother, Big Nurse uses the Indian, but is not of the Indian. Yet the reader also realizes immediately that "those big, womanly breasts" hidden beneath her starched exterior make Big Nurse something other than a bureaucratic automaton. Those breasts eventually, and inevitably, will need to be exposed. For the Chief, Big Nurse is an abstraction, a projection of the symbolic power that stripped his father of his name, but beneath her starched uniform she must also be a reminder of the carnal body of his origins.

McMurphy as Father Figure

For the Chief though, it is clearly not the memory of his mother that gives him any comfort, but the early childhood memories of bonding with his father. When Big Nurse sends the black boys to shave the Chief at the beginning of the novel, for example, the Chief thinks of his father, their hunting trips in the early morning fog in the Dalles. For the Chief it is the father who is associated with the womb-like protection of the fog—a temporary, but ultimately unsatisfying, retreat from the threat of Big Nurse's attempts at symbolic castration. In this opening scene, Big Nurse is clearly in control, forcing the Chief away from any possibility of manhood as "she jams wicker bag and all into Chief Bromden's mouth and shoves it down with a mop handle."

When Randle Patrick McMurphy appears in the ward, however, the Chief is reminded of the strength of his father: "He talks a little the way Papa used to, voice loud and full of hell. . . ." And, as those familiar with the novel know, McMurphy takes on the role of the father for Bromden in order to get Bromden to emerge front the womb-like protection of that fog, to move the Chief to name and remake the father in himself.

Throughout the novel, McMurphy creates strategies (from games to gambling to fishing trips) to get the Chief to understand his full potency, for it is only then that he can name his father. As the Chief finally tells McMurphy, "My Papa was a full Chief and his name was Tee Ah Millatoona. That means The-Pine-That-Stands-Tallest-on-the-Mountain, and we didn't live on a mountain. He was real big when I was a kid. My mother got twice his size." Not surprisingly, shortly after this naming, Big Nurse orders a lobotomy for McMurphy, who is then brought back to the ward, "wheeled in this Gurney with a chart at the bottom that said in heavy black letters, MCMURPHY, RANDLE P. POST-OPERATIVE." Like the Chief's father before him, McMurphy has been symbolically castrated here by a white woman and the white establishment. He has become an impotent member of Big Nurse's symbolic order. Only the abstraction of his name remains, controlled by Big Nurse herself.

In this context, the Chief knows that Big Nurse has silenced McMurphy just as the Combine had silenced his father. Big Nurse can now use McMurphy's name for her own purposes, bringing that name under her authority, making that name part of her matriarchal system. In effect, the same thing had happened to the Chief's father when he married the white woman named Bromden. That name became the family name, the father giving up his authority as the mother continued to grow in size. From the Chief's perspective, these events must have led to his belief that the world was dominated not only by whites, but by a matriarchal structure, one that blocked him from easily rediscovering the manhood embodied within his father. At the same time, the Chief also knows that McMurphy "wouldn't have left something like that sit there in the day room with his name tacked on it for twenty or thirty years so the Big Nurse could use it as an example of what can happen if you buck the system. I was sure of that."

Throughout the novel, the Chief legitimately believes that it is not the name of the father, but Big Nurse, the name of the mother, that defines and represents the ruling symbolic order. His father is "the Other," existing at best at the margins of Big Nurse's discourse, a discourse that the Chief imagines eventually, through his schizophrenic projections, as the abstract order of the Combine itself.

The reader is faced then with a dilemma at the center of Kesey's novel. Not only must the son separate from the mother, but she is being represented within the family romance as the one that needs to be killed, for she is the one who dictates law. The implication, in a larger sense, is that males with fathers of ethnic minority status married to mothers from the dominant culture must travel a difficult and radically indirect route to achieve manhood. In a somewhat confusing pattern, Kesey suggests that sons of "mixed heritage," especially with mothers from the dominant culture, may not be able to achieve manhood in American culture. . . .

Mirroring the Oedipal Conflict

Kesey seems to offer through McMurphy's gestures the joy of the language of the body and of plenitude that McMurphy himself is capable of creating. It is the joyful language that we might imagine the Native American Indian had when he was still close to the natural world, living near the flow of the Columbia River along the Dalles. Such a language is clearly a threat to the rigidity of the symbolic order controlled by Big Nurse. It is the language of "the Other," an articulation of pleasure like the high school carnival that McMurphy discusses with Dr. Spivey, a celebration of polymorphous eroticism[1] that undercuts the monolithic structure of the dominant culture. Most importantly, such a language does not suggest a phallocentric [penis-centered] strategy, but, as [feminist philosopher Hélène] Cixous puts it, a joy of the body that could go on and go on infinitely.

Yet McMurphy also reminds the Chief that a man, like a pine on the tallest mountain (Tee Ah Millatoona), must grow big and stand erect in order to defeat the control of the white matriarchy. And it is this kind of image of phallic power rather than the image of polymorphous eroticism that finally dominates the novel. The Chief's narrative story is filled with the language of play, the poetry of the land, even the playful rhymes of his grandmother. "McMurphy was teaching me. I was feeling better than I'd remembered feeling since I was a kid, when everything was good and the land was still singing kids' poetry to me," the Chief can claim at one point in his story. But in the end the story drives toward a climax and so becomes a plot structured in typical phallocentric terms, undercutting the counter-cultural voice.

1. A Freudian term describing a form of sexual enjoyment not centered in the genitals.

At this level, *Cuckoo's Nest* moves close to the traditional Oedipal narrative concerned with the son's desire to replace the father and gain the phallocentric power as part of his inheritance. Even in this context, however, Kesey makes the narrative problematic. In order to return to his Native American roots, the Chief cannot marry the mother; he must eliminate her. To marry the mother in terms of the Chief's narrative structure would be to lose the name of the father again. In fact, as Kesey has defined the terms of the narrative, there is, ironically, no way for the Chief to achieve manhood without attempting to destroy the mother. For Kesey, marriage is an impossibility. Manhood for the Chief can only be achieved by a frontal attack on Big Nurse.

The climax of McMurphy's battle against Big Nurse then, as it is filtered through the consciousness of the Chief, becomes unfortunately, but by necessity, an act of violence. McMurphy's "red fingers" penetrate "the white flesh of her throat" in an act equivalent to rape; yet there is a hint of how it might have been otherwise as Big Nurse's breasts are for a moment revealed: "the two nippled circles started from her chest and swelled out and out, bigger than anybody had ever imagined, warm and pink in the light. . . ." The image here is of the world of the mother, the feminine body as the Chief would like it to be. But McMurphy's violent attack undercuts such an image, aggravating instead the divisions in the battle of the sexes. Such violence does allow, however, the Chief to attempt to bring to closure his own Oedipal struggle.

When McMurphy is returned to the ward after his lobotomy ordered by Big Nurse, the Chief finally decides to kill him, a killing that not only clearly represents a transfer of sexual energy from McMurphy to the Chief, but also one that signals that the Chief has now assumed the place of McMurphy, his substitute father.

As the Chief describes the killing: "The big, hard body had a tough grip on life. It fought a long time against having it taken away, flailing and thrashing around so much I finally had to lie full length on top of it and scissor the kicking legs with mine while I mashed the pillow into the face. I lay there on top of the body for what seemed days, until the thrashing stopped. Until it was still a while and had shuddered once and was still again. Then I rolled off." In a poignant blending of homoerotic love and death [two basic drives in Freudian theory], the substitute father is sacrificed for the son so that the son can become the father and so preserve the name of the father. But we must still ask: what precisely has the Chief with his mixed heritage gained in this struggle for manhood? And what does he still lack?

In one sense, the Chief has become McMurphy, although he realizes that in some ways he is bigger than McMurphy. McMurphy's cap is too small for him, for example, and the Chief can lift Big Nurse's control panel which McMurphy could not budge. Like McMurphy, the Chief has become a con artist able to survive on the road as he heads for the Columbia Gorge to see "if there's any of the guys (he) used to know back in the village." But if the Chief has saved the name of McMurphy, he has not recovered the place of Tee Ah Milla-toona, nor has he come to terms with his white mother. This is particularly disturbing because, as [critic] Jack Hicks has said, "Kesey suggests repeatedly that memory, knowing one's individual and collective pasts, is a key to any sense of present or future."

Admittedly the Chief has found a voice that allows him to articulate his experience; yet as he says: "It's still hard for me to have a clear mind thinking on it. But it's the truth even if it didn't happen." That "truth" is the burning fear and manic roaring of consciousness that makes up the Chief's own narrative, a narrative that has attempted to unveil through Mc-Murphy the hidden identity of the father. But although we can hear the voice, we cannot locate it any more than the Chief can locate his own father. In fact, the underside of the novel seems to suggest that the Chief, like his father, is part of that culture of Vanishing Americans. The Chief, in other words, may have discovered a voice, but he remains invisible, a man without a name other than that of Bromden. The reader is exposed to the "truth" of the consciousness of the Chief, but the problem is that the reader has nothing to measure that consciousness against. In this sense, the Chief is imprisoned by the "truth" that he has created. He has achieved his individuality, but it is an individuality in isolation.

Kesey Ignores the Central Problem

And here again we can see the contradiction in Kesey's own vision. The Chief's isolation suggests that he has achieved the nineteenth- century version of the American myth of individualism, a myth that Kesey seems to embrace, but one that helped to destroy the Native American. It is a myth about power and about the inability to trust people unless one has control. Kesey's social vision, as we might call it, is bankrupt in such a context. For despite Kesey's good intentions—and that of the counter-culture in general—we see exposed here that the foundation of that vision is not primarily a celebration of social identity or polymorphous erotic pleasure, but rather a further attempt to legitimate male individual identity and phallocentric control.

Where is the Chief when he is telling the story? Unless he has returned to the Cuckoo's Nest, the Chief seems to be living an invisible life outside of that symbolic order that Kesey has defined through Big Nurse as America and that the Chief thinks of as a matriarchy, an extension of his castrating mother. The hope remains, of course, that the Chief will encounter a different style of life at the Columbian Gorge, perhaps becoming the "father" of an alternative culture, but the underside of the tale hints strongly that the Chief really has no place to go, nor is he sure where he is headed. The Chief remains in fact an indeterminate self much like that bluetick hound to which he compares his narrative. "No tracks on the ground but the ones he's making, and he sniffs in every direction with his cold red-rubber nose and picks up no scent but his own fear, fear burning down into him like steam. It's gonna burn me just that way, finally telling about all this. . . ."

The combined issues of mixed heritage and gender definitions leave the reader, and I would suggest, Kesey, stumbling for some sort of satisfying resolution. Yet, there are no clear answers offered within the novel. In the tradition of American fiction Kesey chooses to struggle with these issues but at best only illuminates their complexities. William Faulkner, too, examined these issues in his novel, *Light in August.* Faulkner's main character, Joe Christmas, is like the Chief in that he cannot escape the notion that all women are trying to control and exploit him. He, too, lives in a confused world where the anticipated safety of being male, thereby dominant in a patriarchy, is denied him because of his mixed heritage and his consequential understanding of social order as a matriarchy.

In seeking resolution both authors ignore the primary cause of the conflict: mixed heritage. They neglect to have their characters personally challenge the system of oppression which labels a minority male as beneath a white female, another victim of the oppressive system. Instead, they skirt the issue, each allowing his main character to regain his manhood simply by claiming it with a six word phrase. Joe Christmas, tired of being a passenger on the roller-coaster of life declares his intention to take control with, "I am going to do something." While the Chief announces his reentry into manhood with the powerful words, "I been away a long time." . . .

Critics such as Robert Forrey have attacked Kesey claiming that he is sexist. Forrey, for example, places Kesey in the machismo tradition of [Ernest] Hemingway and [John] Steinbeck: " . . . what we have in Kesey's novel is yet another group of American males trying desperately to unite into a quasi-religious cult or brotherhood which will enable them to sublimate their homosexuality in violent athletic contests, gambling, or other forms of psychopathological horseplay." But Forrey's important insight is only half the story.

Kesey has given us the vision of a half-breed, a man of color rooted in a mixed heritage, and he has asked the question—how does such a person, with a dominant white mother, achieve manhood within a heterosexual arrangement? Kesey has begun to explore that question in *Cuckoo's Nest*, but he has failed to understand that such issues of gender and race need to include the insidious structures of patriarchy in their analysis. At the same time, though, the questions that he raises remain important ones, and so reflect the relevance and the uniqueness of Kesey's vision for us today.

Kesey Critiques a Society That Uses Fear and Conformity to Emasculate Men

Michael Meloy

Michael Meloy received a PhD from the University of South Carolina and has taught literature classes at Stevenson University in Maryland.

In the following article, Meloy contends that One Flew over the Cuckoo's Nest *needs to be understood in the context of the Cold War era in which it was written. A climate of fear and conformity characterized the era, and writers such as Ken Kesey reacted to this climate by creating narratives with macho figures who battle fiercely against a sterile society. The inmates in* One Flew over the Cuckoo's Nest *have all been emasculated, and McMurphy attempts to restore potency to them. Meloy suggests that McMurphy is not wholly successful and that at the end of the novel the masculinity of the inmates is still in jeopardy.*

In our current political climate, where foreign policy decisions often utilize a gendered rhetoric that seems to reflect an obsession with ensuring our national vitality and virility, Kesey's criticism of a cold-war society that he believed fundamentally emasculated men strikes a chord in contemporary America. Randall P. McMurphy's brief stint in a mental hospital, where he persuades the submissive male patients to rise up against ruthless, emasculating Nurse Ratched, is a story replete with issues of particular immediacy in contemporary America: heightened surveillance, the corruption of administration, the degradation of the individual, and a fundamental terror of perceived feminization. . . .

Michael Meloy, "Fixing Men: Castration, Impotence, and Masculinity in Ken Kesey's *One Flew over the Cuckoo's Nest*," *The Journal of Men's Studies*, vol. 17, no. 1, Winter 2009, pp. 3–14. Copyright © 2009 by the Men's Studies Press. All rights reserved. Reproduced by permission.

Masculinity in the Cold War Fifties

The central argument of this essay posits that Kesey was one of a number of figures who formed a primal, virility-centered conception of masculinity as a subtle response to the political climate of the McCarthy era.[1] Kesey's fictional rebellion in the mental ward—his heroic characterization and victimization of the inmates and his analogous demonization of the institution and its representative, Nurse Ratched—responds to a cold war age of overwhelming surveillance and fear. The demeaning and callous nature of the administration's treatment of the inmates symbolizes a national government that, in Kesey's view, acted likewise. At Menlo Park, [California,] where Kesey worked as an orderly in the mid-1950s, he began to see a group of men alienated from a cold-war social system that destabilizes their sense of self. In an interview, Kesey explains that the experience gave him "a sense that maybe [the inmates] were not so crazy or as bad as the sterile environment they were living in."

In *One Flew Over the Cuckoo's Nest*, these themes of control, submission, and alienation link to gender, representing similar fears of female empowerment and a male power rendered impotent by a sterile social structure. In the postwar era, the discourse of gender and sexuality was, indeed, culturally linked to the political climate of surveillance. . . .

This culture of fear that pervaded the cultural landscape of the cold- war fifties took on homosexual and gender connotations. While McCarthy warned Americans that they were becoming "pink," Freudian theories that circulated widely in the decade similarly warned Americans that they were all latent homosexuals, and [sex researcher] Alfred Kinsey's *Sexual Behavior in the Human Male* suggested that many more American men either performed homosexual acts or thought about

1. Senator Joseph McCarthy created a climate of paranoia in early 1950s America by claiming that the major U.S. institutions had been infiltrated by Communists. He held hearings to find these persons that soon became little more than a witch hunt.

performing homosexual acts. Kinsey's work undermined traditional notions of normative sexuality, contributing to a national obsession with homosexuality and placing sexual preference and performance at the forefront of the public's perception of manhood. . . .

The fiction of the 1950s and 1960s reflects this cultural phenomenon of the early Cold War, often featuring an angry defensive male figure who finds his manhood threatened and retaliates through a violent sexual act. Where modernist male heroes often lacked sexual virility, post–World War 2 writers tended to privilege virility and promote sexual and emotional release rather than restraint. Their characters are more animalistic, more virile and lustful, and increasingly antagonistic to a social network that is often portrayed as feminine or feminizing. James Dickey's *Deliverance* features this point of view, as does the work of Norman Mailer and William Styron. The increased representation of violent sexual acts in their works is linked to an evolving masculine identity that re-emphasized an essentialist conception of gender, in which gender criteria are believed to be biologically determined rather than socially constructed, thus associating manhood with virility and a male need for sexual release. . . .

Castration or Lobotomy?

One Flew Over the Cuckoo's Nest features both a masculine hero who is able to transform his masculine performance in front of different audiences and a male patient (Billy Bibbit) who is encouraged to reassert his masculinity via sexual performance—a performance validated by the witnessing of the other patients, who laugh approvingly as they look on. That both these attempts fail, leading to Billy's suicide and McMurphy's lobotomy, confronts readers of Kesey's novel with a fundamental choice that, for Kesey, reflects the crisis of masculinity in the postwar era: castration or lobotomy. The men who repress their sexuality, and consequently their innate masculinity are psychologically castrated, whereas the rest are sacrificed.

These issues of male sexuality are invoked as early as the opening of the novel, where the narrator announces that "[b]lack boys in white suits . . . commit sex acts in the hall," indicating that sexual release must be obtained subversively. After the first Group Therapy meeting, the persecution of the patients becomes linked to castration, where McMurphy immediately implicates Nurse Ratched, calling her "a bitch and a buzzard and a ballcutter," then adding,

> [T]he best way . . . to get you to knuckle under is to weaken you by gettin' you where it hurts the worst . . . go for your vitals. And that's what the old buzzard is doing, going for your vitals.

McMurphy's fear of castration here is both gendered and specific to the ward. According to McMurphy, the men's vitals are in danger and Nurse Ratched wields the knife. McMurphy, who directly associates psychological power with sexual power, sees his "vitals" as the core of his masculine power. McMurphy's reference to her as an "old Buzzard" subtly besmirches feminine power as something degrading and shameful—residing at the bottom of the food chain, feeding off of dead carcasses. Furthermore, Kesey implies that, under the guise of this feminine power, masculine identity can only exist in a decayed and rotting state.

At the same time, it's important to recognize the way in which the danger to masculine sexuality does not reside solely in the aggressive feminine force. Rather, Nurse Ratched encompasses a larger social system. McMurphy says, "I've seen a thousand of 'em, old and young, men and women. Seen 'em all over the country and in the homes—people who try to make you weak . . .". Contemporary life itself becomes something that weakens men by "getting [them] where it hurts the worst."

Instead, the evil force in *One Flew Over the Cuckoo's Nest* is what Bromden calls "the combine," the systematic societal machine that transforms women into cold unfeeling robots like Ratched and men into submissive rabbits like Harding. In that sense, Kesey creates a ward that he sees as a microcosm for a society that systematically castrates men by suppressing their sexual impulse. Again, Kesey's critique of a feminizing postwar culture parallels similar national concerns. In an era where many Americans worried about an emasculating nation state, Kesey's own reaction roughly coincided with a common national reaction, in which Americans embraced a bolder sexually aggressive, promiscuous, heterosexual male.

Indeed, the patients on Nurse Ratched's ward—a representation of an American culture that has allowed men's sexual impulses to be repressed—have all failed somehow in their sexual exploits. In Group Therapy, for example, Harding's marital problems begin to have sexual implications when we discover that he "may give her reason to seek further sexual attention" elsewhere. Harding has been thoroughly feminized by the women around him, and is described by Bromden as "too pretty to just be a guy on the street" with "hands so long and white and dainty." Likewise, Billy's obsession with his mother prevents him from having relationships with other women. When Billy reveals his plans to marry someday, his mother laughs at the idea, telling him, "Sweetheart, you still have scads of time for things like that." Indeed, we find that almost all of the patients are on the ward because of troubled relationships with women. . . . Even the male staffers that work in the ward find themselves emasculated, seemingly by the very presence of Nurse Ratched. Bromden describes the common complaint of doctors after they have been on the ward for a while: "Since I started on that ward with that woman I feel like my veins are running ammonia. I shiver all the time, my kids won't sit in my lap, my wife won't sleep with me . . .".

In this way, the ward becomes characterized as a sexual desert, full of decaying men with increased sexual problems and who are consistently characterized by the narrator as feminine. We are told the men gossip, giggle, and "snicker in their fists." The predominant feature of this feminization becomes submissiveness, a trait that can be seen in Kesey's description of the inmates while working at the psychiatric ward in Menlo Park. . . .

McMurphy Is Masculinized

Kesey contrasts such victimized males with Bromden's overt masculinization of McMurphy. According to the Chief, McMurphy is "big" and he "talks like papa . . . loud and full of hell." In addition, McMurphy's sideburns, his devilish grin, and his iron-heeled boots give him a tough John Wayne persona that encourages readers to associate him with hard masculinity:

> He's got on work-farm pants and shirt, sunned out till they're the color of watered milk. His face and neck and arms are the color of oxblood leather from working long in the fields. He's got a primer-black motorcycle cap stuck in his hair and a leather jacket over one arm, and he's got on boots gray and dusty and heavy enough to kick a man in two.

As here, the Chief's impressions of McMurphy always emphasize strength and toughness, positing a working man's body with a rough exterior. McMurphy's body is hard, "kind of the way a baseball is hard under the scuffed leather".

Furthermore, McMurphy's sexual potency is emphasized from the very first Group Therapy meeting, where we find out McMurphy is a sexual predator, having been convicted of statutory rape. McMurphy's defense specifically reveals his own sexual power: "she was plenty willin' . . . so willin', in fact, that I took to sewing my pants shut." That is, McMurphy's sexual drive becomes his own defense, implying that short of

Louise Fletcher (as Nurse Ratched) and Brad Dourif (as Billy Bibbit) in a scene from the 1975 film adaptation of Ken Kesey's One Flew over the Cuckoo's Nest. *United Artists/ Fantasy Films/The Kobal Collection/The Picture Desk, Inc.*

"sewing [his] pants shut," there is nothing a man can do to stop himself. That is, the male sexual impulse cannot be controlled, to the point where he suggests that she "would of actually burnt me to a frazzle."

When McMurphy, who represents the masculine ideal in the novel because of his virile power, discovers that his file indicates "repeated outbreaks of passion," he mocks the possibility that being "overzealous in . . . sexual relations" is a serious problem. McMurphy's character, centered on his sexuality, is dependent on others' perception of him as an overly sexual being.

Feminine Sexuality and Empowerment

Without sexual license, the novel seems to argue, the masculine self cannot cope with the feminine other. Indeed, Bromden's descriptions of Ratched point to a fear of the nurse shared by most of the acute patients, particularly when the Chief catches a glimpse of what he takes to be the Nurse's "hideous real self." Bromden's description, in which "she blows up bigger and bigger, big as a tractor," indicates a terror of the nurse that recurs numerous times in the novel. Harding's admission in Group Therapy that "his wife's ample bosom . . . gives him a feeling of inferiority" seems to function in a similar way. In the face of his own sexual impotency, Harding cannot help but subordinate himself to a female sexual power that intimidates him. Conversely, the prostitutes of the novel exist in a purely sexual way, making them less terrifying, and, in that sense, *One Flew Over the Cuckoo's Nest* seems to privilege Candy and Ginger because they are prostitutes. Their sexual availability encourages men to release their innate sexuality. Unlike the prostitutes, Nurse Ratched hides her enormous breasts, represses her feminine sexuality, which the novel seems to disapprove of. . . .

The antagonism in the novel toward feminine power—a mysterious and alluring force that inevitably proves destructive to men—can be better understood in the context of the postwar era, where women in numerous sectors of the economy refused to return to the home when men returned from World War Two. As Joanne Meyerowitz's collection [*Not June Cleaver: Women and Gender in Post War America*] aptly demonstrates, the fifties was, for women, a period of increased independence and rising feminism, a trend that Kesey's work seems to recognize. Furthermore, Kesey's work represents a larger cultural fear that, as women move into more powerful positions, men will become emasculated. . . .

For McMurphy to retain his masculinity, then, some sexual act needs to be performed, a sexual conquest must be attained. Because the other patients' essential lack is a sexual outlet, McMurphy believes that satisfying this masculine sex drive will provide a resolution—will liberate them once again. When McMurphy asks for vitamins from one of the nurses, saying he's "getting" them for Billy Boy," he subtly denigrates Billy's sexual virility while also implying that a sexual and psychological awakening is coming. McMurphy tells the nurse that Billy "seems to have a peaked look of late" and adds, "I thought I'd wait till about midnight when he'd have the most need for them." At first, it seems as if sneaking Candy on to the ward will satisfy this sexual urge, as McMurphy's sexual innuendo suggests: "[T]hey checked my plugs and cleaned my points, and I got a glow on like a Model T spark coil." At the same time, it is assumed that the opportunity to "cash in [Billy's] cherry" will make a man out of him. Even Turkle, the night watchman, seems to approve of McMurphy's intent, willing to let the prostitutes into the ward so long as he gets to satisfy his sexual desires as well. "You people be sharing more'n a bottle, won't you," Turkle asks with a grin.

In a very important way, however, sexual acts with Candy and Ginger cannot suffice. These are not the female figures that terrorize McMurphy and the ward. Rather, McMurphy must retain his masculinity by confronting the female figure of power. McMurphy must rape Nurse Ratched. Thus, when McMurphy finally attacks Nurse Ratched toward the end of the novel, nearly killing her, it symbolically (but also in a disturbingly literal way) represents a sexual assault. Sexual restraint and denial culminate here, in an act in which violence and sexuality converge:

> After he'd smashed through that glass door, her face swinging around, with terror forever ruining any other look she might ever try to use again, screaming when he grabbed for her and ripped her uniform all the way down the front, screaming again when the two nippled circles started from her chest and swelled out and out, bigger than anybody had ever imagined, warm and pink in the light.

Violence itself becomes a kind of sex act here—one that drains Nurse Ratched of her power and transforms her from the cold mother figure into the prostitute. McMurphy exposes her feminine sexuality, revealing the "two nippled circles"—a literal transformation here from a cold machine to something more vulnerable, something "warm and pink." In addition, McMurphy transfers the terror that Nurse Ratched inspired in the patients into terror that Nurse Ratched herself feels.

Nurse Ratched's fear empowers the men, but the result is not particularly satisfying. By exposing Ratched, McMurphy essentially exposes himself as the evasive calf whom Kesey described as having "too much spirit to be a steer." Because Ratched is simply a cog in a larger social system that feminizes men, McMurphy's act was a sacrificial one, and the ensuing lobotomy of McMurphy offers us a succinct and powerful metaphor for Kesey's vision of the masculine condition. Men who cannot properly repress their sexual urges in this new environment will inevitably be sacrificed. Those that cannot be castrated will indeed be lobotomized. In this way, McMurphy's sacrificial lobotomy allows Bromden to see that he too is faced with a choice. Bromden observes during shock therapy, "They got the dice loaded to throw a snake eyes . . . and I'm the load," suggesting a metaphor for his future, both culturally and in terms of gender. Playing the game entails putting himself in a losing position—inevitably crapping out.

Note, however, that either scenario entails the danger of castration. To remain in the ward, safe from a feminizing society, is to go the way of McMurphy or Harding. On the other hand, to escape the ward means escaping Nurse Ratched's knife, but requires facing an emasculating society. For Bromden, gender identity combines with cultural identity, and to re-establish both, Bromden must confront the cultural system that oppresses him. That is, Bromden must face a civilization that he has spent the novel fleeing. In that sense, Bromden's escape, as well as the physical act of lifting the tub to break the window and escape the ward, becomes a symbolic act—an assertion of his masculine self. In addition, Bromden describes the event in religious terms, saying that "the glass splashed out in the moon, like a bright cold water baptizing the sleeping earth," giving the act an almost spiritual meaning.

Kesey's ending here is not simply an assertion of masculine freedom, but instead a much more ambiguous, and perhaps even pessimistic move. By essentially ending the novel in the ward, Kesey refuses to allow the reader to witness the success or failure of the patients in the outside world. To end in this manner indicates Kesey's refusal to provide a resolution where he sees none existing. Rather, Kesey sees masculinity as still very much endangered here.

This refusal on Kesey's part to resolve the gender issues he has presented says much about his perception of masculinity in a world of McCarthy hearings and atom bombs. On one hand, *One Flew Over the Cuckoo's Nest* can be interpreted as a kneejerk reaction to an increasingly aggressive feminist force, and a perceived loss of masculine empowerment (by modernization as much as femininity). However, it's important to recognize that works like *One Flew Over the Cuckoo's Nest* were catalysts for the sexual revolution of the 1960s. After Kesey published it, he started a counterculture movement that lasted well over a decade. The free love hippie movement that exploded in the late 1960s had some of its seedlings planted here, in characters like McMurphy, who advocates open sexuality and freedom of sexual expression. This ideology defined Kesey's early career, locating the masculine self in a primal, instinctual sexual drive that he believed men impulsively seek to satisfy.

In any period of high-capitalism, identity itself becomes a consumable product, a commodity to be marketed, bought, and sold. The sexualizing of heterosexual masculinity in the fiction, film, and magazines of the period commodifies a masculine identity that could cope with perceived threats of homosexuality. Ken Kesey combined with figures like Norman Mailer, [Playboy empire founder] Hugh Hefner, and [James Bond's creator] Ian Fleming, all of whom created masculine personas that offered the American public the possibility of avoiding being labeled "pink," by taking up acts deemed heterosexual. Exhibiting an open, exaggerated sexuality became an opportunity to validate one's heterosexuality. Conversely, to not participate in the sexual rhetoric of Joe McCarthy, [author] Mickey Spillane, and Ian Fleming was to potentially render oneself unmanly.

This seems especially prevalent today, where globalization would seem to further increase the commodification of the individual. American culture today is inundated with sexuality, where masculinity has become an industry unto itself and where, perhaps more than ever before in American history, sexual behavior marks one's identity. Signs and symbols encouraging sexual expression surround us, and men's magazines from the fifties, such as *Playboy* and *Esquire*, have spawned a hundred others. In that sense, Kesey's work exhibits a masculinity that can perhaps help us understand the obsession with masculine sexual virility and violence in our own time, a new age in which male sexuality has become, like so many other things, a product of conspicuous consumption.

Social Issues in Literature

CHAPTER 3

Contemporary Perspectives on Mental Illness

People with Severe Mental Illness Can Live Productively in Society

Kate Sheppard

Kate Sheppard is a political reporter for Grist *magazine.*

While many people with severe mental illness shuttle back and forth among homeless centers, outplacement treatment centers, and state psychiatric hospitals, there are some innovative programs that treat people so effectively that they are able to return to normal society, according to Sheppard in the following article. Fountain House in New York City is such a program. Sheppard reports that it succeeds in its goal of getting patients with mental illness out of homeless shelters and hospitals and back into society by helping them develop social and coping skills and preparing them for employment. Fountain House far exceeds national statistics for getting its clients employed and also delivers its services at a significantly lower cost than do more traditional methods.

Nehemiah Surratt delivers the mail every morning at the Dow Jones office near Times Square in Manhattan. He sorts the incoming mail, transports it to the various departments, and picks up outgoing documents. In the afternoon, Surratt takes classes at Hunter College, where he's a straight-A student majoring in Spanish translation. Soft-spoken and shy, dressed in a rumpled, gray button-down shirt and a white knit cap, Surratt could be any other 26-year-old making his way in the world.

Two years ago, he scraped up all his savings and flew to New York, where he planned to kill himself in a cheap Mid-

Kate Sheppard, "Programs That Work," *The American Prospect*, vol. 19, no. 7, July/August 2008, pp. A15–17. Copyright © 2008 The American Prospect, Inc. All rights reserved. Reproduced with permission from *The American Prospect*, 11 Beacon Street, Suite 1120, Boston, MA 02108.

town motel. He'd never been to the city before, he says, and he wanted to see it before he died.

"I stayed for three days, spent all my money," Surratt says. "I ended up changing my mind, because I looked out the window and I saw how beautiful the city was and decided I should get help."

A Different Kind of Program

He went to a homeless shelter, and eventually a caseworker there referred him to the state psychiatric hospital, where he stayed for a month and a half. Doctors determined that he suffered from severe depression, which Surratt now says had plagued him since middle school. After being discharged, he bounced between his hometown of Norfolk, Virginia, and homeless shelters in New York, finding and losing jobs, spending time in out-patient treatment centers, and passing from caseworker to caseworker.

As it does for many individuals with severe mental illness, this might have become the story of the rest of Surratt's life— unemployed, homeless, cut off from others, and trapped in a system that offers few opportunities for exit. Yet, unlike many individuals with severe mental illness, Surratt found his way to Fountain House, an innovative program in Manhattan that helps individuals with severe mental illness transition out of the broken system and back to work, school, and the greater community through a special model of recovery called the Clubhouse program.

The price of the nation's broken mental-health system is high for people like Surratt, and for the nation itself. Each year, 5 million to 6 million Americans aged 16 to 54 lose, fail to seek, or cannot find employment because of a mental illness. At least 200,000 Americans with mental illness are homeless, and another 200,000 are in the criminal-justice system. Those who aren't homeless or institutionalized are often confined to their homes and isolated from society. But Clubhouses, as well as other recovery-oriented, community-based options like Assertive Community Treatment (ACT) programs, offer real promise for individuals with mental illness, while at the same time saving millions of dollars for state and local governments.

Only a generation ago, individuals with mental illness were likely to end up in state psychiatric hospitals. But in recent decades, as lawmakers favored "deinstitutionalization," many such facilities were shuttered and the patients returned to their communities. Funding for community-based mental-health programs was supposed to follow but has been inadequate, leaving many of the mentally ill consigned to nursing homes or, worse, the streets. In addition, tight budgets for mental health and an unwillingness to depart from traditional clinical models have crippled the growth of well-established, community-based programs like Clubhouse and ACT, making them available to only a fraction of people living with mental illness.

Emphasis on Building Relationships

Unlike traditional programs for people with severe mental illnesses like schizophrenia, bipolar disorder, and major depression, Fountain House is a voluntary program with the goal of getting people like Surratt out of homeless shelters and hospitals and back into society. Fountain House was founded as the world's first Clubhouse in 1948 by six men who had been discharged from Rockland State Psychiatric Center and sought a place where individuals like them could find a community to support their recovery and help them develop life skills.

Sixty years later, Fountain House serves some 350 people each day, and up to 1,500 visit each month. It now also houses a training program, where people can come to learn how to start Clubhouses in their communities, as well as the International Center for Clubhouse Development (ICCD), an organization that works to promote, train, and support Clubhouses around the world. ICCD has helped the model expand to 326 Clubhouses in 29 countries serving 55,000 people a day, with 220 Clubhouses in the United States alone.

Proponents of the model cast it as a social movement rather than a program or service, and individuals who join the Clubhouse are "members" instead of patients or clients. Clubhouse members select a staff worker who serves as their advocate, working with them to achieve a personalized plan and goals. There are no clinical services offered within the Clubhouse, but staffers refer members to appropriate psychiatric and medical care and housing, employment, and education services. The emphasis within the Clubhouse, though, is not on an individual's illness but on his or her interests and goals.

A high value is placed on equity among members and staff, and all tasks—from scrubbing toilets to serving on the board of directors—are shared. Members participate in all the day-to-day operations of the Clubhouse as part of a work unit, which in most Clubhouses includes dining-hall, clerical, education, and employment units. As the largest Clubhouse in the world, Fountain House offers a wider range of work units, and on any given weekday, members tend to the garden in the horticulture unit, write articles for the newsletter in the clerical unit, and help plan classes about managing diabetes in the wellness unit.

In addition to the day's work, most Clubhouse members can also attend classes for things like computing and exercise, as well as evening and weekend social events. Most Clubhouses also offer a subsidized daily lunch and holiday meals. Through work and social engagement, members are able to develop relationships with each other and staff members, who can help them deal with the many challenges of living with mental illness.

"The priority is building strong relationships . . . that can empower members and help them pursue their recovery

The author of the viewpoint mentions Fountain House as one organization that enables people dealing with mental illness to function successfully in society. The building in New York City, pictured here, is the original Fountain House, after which many programs have been modeled worldwide. Photograph by Leslie Barbaro, courtesy of Fountain House, New York, NY.

goals," says Joel Corcoran, executive director of the ICCD. "The entire focus is on what you can accomplish, whereas in the traditional medical model the focus is on what your disability is."

Productive Members of Society

Beyond developing coping and social skills, the Clubhouse also helps prepare members for independent employment or education. After securing commitments from local employers, Clubhouse staff go to the job site, learn the job, and then teach the needed skills to a Clubhouse member, who will hold the position for six to nine months. If the member hits a bump in the road, a Clubhouse staffer or colleague will cover for him. The model benefits the businesses because they are guaranteed coverage in an entry-level, high-turnover position.

And the arrangement is a win-win for the new worker, allowing him to gain valuable work experience and build a resume while learning to manage his illness. Members in transitional employment work 12 to 20 hours each week, and earn above minimum wage. Fountain House members are employed in such prominent New York businesses as Dow Jones, McGraw Hill, and the American Stock Exchange, where they work as mail clerks, as messengers, and in food service, for instance. After the initial placement, members can opt for a second transitional post or work with a staff member to secure independent "supported" employment, while others may pursue a GED [high school diploma] or a college degree.

By all of these important measures, the Clubhouse model has demonstrated solid success. Though only 15 percent of individuals with severe mental illness are employed nationally, 40 percent of Clubhouse members are in transitional or supported employment at any given time. Over a 30-month period of membership, 60 percent of Clubhouse participants have been employed. And those who aren't in jobs are generally in school or working toward employment. These figures are even more impressive in light of the fact that four in 10 Clubhouse members originally said they had no interest in employment, often because they believed they were unemployable. Within one year of membership, half of that group is engaged in an employment program through the Clubhouse.

"The very way we define ourselves in Western culture is about our productivity," says Pauline Anderson, development director for the ICCD. "Most people living with a serious mental illness, despite what they're told by their physicians or by society, want to be productive citizens, want to be productive members of society, want to go back to work."

In addition to providing opportunities for members, Clubhouses also have proven benefits for the states that support them. Communities spend an average $657 per day of hospitalization for individuals with mental illness, while the costs of Clubhouses total just $27.42 per day. A number of studies have found that the opportunities offered through Clubhouses significantly decrease both hospitalization and incarceration rates for members and increase the number of members living in independent housing rather than shelters or group homes, at a great savings to the states that support them.

The ACT Program

Another approach that has proven highly successful for people with serious mental illness is the Program of Assertive Community Treatment, also known as PACT or ACT. Much like the Clubhouse model, ACT programs are intended to help individuals re-enter society through housing, education, and employment. ACT was designed by a team of doctors at Mendota State Hospital in Madison, Wisconsin, in the 1960s as a way to provide treatment for individuals with mental illness within their own community.

ACT services are deployed through a mobile, multidisciplinary team of 10 to 12 trained professionals. Many teams also include a substance-abuse counselor and a "peer support" specialist—someone who has experienced mental illness firsthand and can provide advocacy and guidance. In more traditional models of outpatient care, individuals are assigned to separate case managers, psychiatrists, medical doctors, and housing and employment services, which often creates a fragmented and unstable system of care. But an ACT team consists of professionals in each of those areas who can provide services 24 hours a day, 365 days a year.

The model is intended to flex to the needs of individual users, often called "consumers" or "clients." Team members collaborate to create a treatment plan and coordinate with each other to ensure that the consumer's needs are being met. If the client is facing a mental-health crisis, a team member will accompany him to the hospital. If he decides to seek a job, the team's vocational counselor will work with him to achieve that goal as well.

"It helps people live independently who might have their life much more controlled in institutions," says Elizabeth Edgar, a senior policy analyst at the National Alliance on Mental Illness (NAMI), which supports the development of ACT programs. Like Clubhouses, the goal of ACT is to help individuals with severe mental illness acclimate to life in the community and be able to access the range of opportunities available to everyone else. "It's a way for a person to reclaim things that they may have given up on, like going back to college, working, or living [on their own]," Edgar says.

Because of its mobility and flexibility, ACT is also a model that can reach those who are most disabled by mental illness, or who are homeless or even incarcerated. The approach allows for individualized, person-centered care, says Cheri Sixbey, executive director of the Assertive Community Treatment Association (ACTA), an organization that provides support and training for ACT teams. It also allows individuals with mental illness to recover within their own community, among relatives, friends, and neighbors. "It's honoring community and seeing people as more than a mental-health patient," says Sixbey, who is a former ACT program manager from Livingston, Michigan.

ACT teams are in place in at least 35 states, though they are more widely available and better funded in some places than in others. Michigan alone has 100 teams, and other states, like New Jersey, Indiana, and Oklahoma have increased their investment in these programs over recent years. Fifteen states, however, have no ACT program at all.

Programs Save Money

Like the Clubhouse model, the ACT approach has a proven record of success. National surveys found that ACT participants spent 78 percent fewer days in the hospital than individuals in other outpatient programs, while other research found an 83 percent reduction in the number of days spent in jail by program participants. In Georgia alone, reduced hospitalization and incarceration of individuals receiving ACT services saved the state $1.1 million in a single year. Nationally, ACT participants were also much more likely to be employed; within 30 months of joining, 74 percent of them had secured a job.

Cost-effectiveness aside, community-based programs like ACT and Clubhouse should be supported because they are more socially just than traditional medical-care models, says Robert Bernstein, executive director of the David L. Bazelon Center for Mental Health Law, an organization that advocates for the rights of individuals with mental illness. "These are fellow citizens who have disabilities and who have quite a bit to offer society," Bernstein says. "People want to have a job, they want to own something, to have a life, and not just simply be treated as a former mental patient."

Within the consumer-rights movement, some argue that programs like ACT and Clubhouse don't go far enough in being recovery-based and self-determined. According to Dan Fisher, executive director of the National Empowerment Center, a coalition of consumer-advocacy groups, these programs still involve an over-reliance on professional staff and medical treatment. There should be a wider range of opportunities available to individuals living with mental illness, and more peer-driven programs. Fisher points to states like Florida and Oregon, where individuals with mental illness can select from a range of community-based options, and the funding follows.

But securing funding to develop and sustain even model initiatives like ACT or Clubhouse is often difficult, says NAMI executive director Michael Fitzpatrick. "The tragedy in America is if you look at our mental-health system, in most states and counties there's really . . . a lack of political will to fund these very innovative, effective programs."

Many policy-makers simply assume that traditional institutional or clinical care models are cheaper, despite the demonstrable cost savings that the government accrues from programs like ACT and Clubhouse. Making the case for these models is also hampered by the absence of studies that quantify the full costs of untreated or mistreated mental illness across the whole system-from hospitalization and incarceration to the cost of dispatching police officers to deal with mental-health emergencies or transport homeless individuals.

The structure of the funding system for mental health in this country also works against programs like Clubhouse and ACT. Sixty percent of funding for mental-health programs comes from state and county governments, and it is often difficult to convince legislators or health departments to fund new programs, especially in states where budgets are already tight. In some states, like Illinois, individuals with mental illness are often assigned to nursing homes, and legislative efforts to shift funding from those nursing homes to community-based care programs have met stiff resistance from the nursing-home industry and other entrenched interests.

"There are vested interests in the status quo," says Robert Bernstein, who also cites the influence of the nursing-home industry. The result is a system that throws all of its money at crisis situations rather than investing in long-term, recovery-based programs. "We really do have the [knowledge] to help people" with severe mental illness, Bernstein notes. "We're just not doing it for political reasons."

Psychosurgery Raises Ethical Issues

Lauren Slater

Lauren Slater is a psychologist in Somerville, Massachusetts. She is the author of Opening Skinner's Box, *among other books.*

Psychosurgery has been around since the 1930s, but it was largely abandoned in the 1960s, when public opinion turned against the procedure as reports of abuses and botched operations became known. In the following selection, Slater reports that advances are being made in a procedure that places electrodes in the brain. This psychosurgery is being used in some areas for patients whose psychiatric problems are severe and do not respond to more conventional treatment. Although initial success rates hold out promise, Slater raises ethical issues surrounding this operation. In her opinion, it places inordinate control of a human's emotional state in the hands of a physician.

Mario Della Grotta is 35 years old, with a shaved head and a tattoo of a rose on his pumped left shoulder. He wears gold rings on three of his beefy fingers and a gold chain around his neck. His neck is as thick as a thigh, and strong, and beneath the skin lie the raised ridges of what look like veins but are really wires from his surgery. He's the kind of guy you might picture on a Cessna 140, speeding down the highway with no helmet, or in a bar in a working-class Italian section of town in the afternoon, a cigarette wedged in the corner of his lip and a shot glass full of something amber. He is the kind of guy who looks tough and would seem, on first appearance, to swagger his way through the world, but that is not true of Mario. For the past 14 years, Mario has had such severe anxiety that, three years ago, his psychiatrist, Ben Green-berg of Butler Hospital in Providence, R.I., suggested psycho-surgery, or what, in the current medical climate, is now being labeled neuro-surgery for psychiatric disorders. Mario couldn't stop counting and checking. In his attempts to ward off panic, rituals consumed 18 hours of his days. Fearful of dirt, he had to take three showers. He searched for symmetries. His formal diagnosis was obsessive-compulsive disorder [OCD], which is just a fancy way of saying scared. Was the car door locked? Did he count that up correctly? The French call obsessive-compulsive disorder *mania de doubte*, a much more apt title than our clinical OCD; *mania de doubte*, a phrase that gets to the existential core of worry, the difficulties of gracefully giv-ing up the ground, opting instead for a clenched, demonic doubting that overrides evidence, empiricism, plain common sense. For Mario, life was crammed into a single, serrated question mark.

Improved Psychosurgery Techniques

Since 1935 at least, psychosurgery has been used to treat anxi-ety disorders like OCD and its close cousin, melancholy, but it has always involved destroying neural tissue. It has involved cutting whole nerve tracts between here and there, taking down the phone lines. Forty, 50 years ago, any benefits people derived from the knife were perilously balanced against the flattening of feeling and the blanching of their personalities. Now, however, this is no longer true. Pacemakers for the brain, originally developed to treat movement disorders in Parkinson's patients, are beginning to be used on some of the most intractable but common psychiatric problems: anxiety, and depression. Still highly experimental and available only to patients for whom every other available treatment has failed, the implants nevertheless suggest a time in the not-too-distant future when there may be options other than drugs for both those disorders. Given the current suspicions regarding the safety and efficacy of SSRIs (selective serotonin reuptake inhibitors), we need those other options. Soon, we may have a whole new cure on our hands, and in our heads. . . .

In fact, neural implants are not new; they are merely being revived. Among the first researchers to experiment with the use of implants in the treatment of psychiatric cases was Robert Heath, who implanted over 100 electrodes in patients over a series of six years. This was back in the 1950s, when psychosurgery was still an industry. Heath was a handsome man with a spade-shaped beard and elegant hands, and he worked at the Tulane University School of Medicine, which was not far from the back wards of Louisiana's mental hospitals and prisons, places of high, coiled wire: black, lacy grates: and unremitting sunlight. Heath took criminals, slit open their skulls, dropped electrodes down deep inside them, and then, with the use of a handheld stimulator, waited to see what would happen. Here's what happened: Heath discovered that electrodes placed in the medial forebrain bundle, otherwise known as the septal area of the brain, produced feelings of intense pleasure, while electrodes inserted into the tegmentum made a man enraged. Electrodes placed just so in the amygdala produced feelings of fear or its alternate, calmness, depending on the setting. Writes Heath, "The possibility of ameliorating or even curing psychiatric conditions through the use of these implants is vast." Heath, along with José Delgado at the Yale University School of Medicine, found that they could stimulate and snuff anxiety with the small flip of a switch: they could take shy animals and make them social, and take social animals and make them shy; they could induce fear and reduce fear. And it all seemed so easy. Heath treated a homosexual man by implanting an electrode in his pleasure center and then having him watch movies of heterosexual encounters, and within 12 sessions, he was a newly made man. The patient proved it to Heath by sleeping with a prostitute on a hot Louisiana night, when even the walls were sweating, and he was successful.

Neural implants were significant right from the start, not only because they provided hope for the clinically distressed, but also because they, in part, changed the way we collectively thought of the brain. Prior to Heath and others before him, like Wilder Penfield and Paul Broca, many people believed thoughts and emotions were carried by blood through our heads via hollow tunnels. Once researchers like Heath demonstrated, however, that you could prod a tiny piece of cortical tissue and get a specific response—a taste of prune in the mouth, a smear of yellow in the air—Broca's theory of localization was confirmed. This was a major mind shift, the brain now a series of discrete centers that, when wiped out, could cause tremendous loss and, when stimulated, could make many things froth forth.

Neural implants were abandoned in the 1960s, when the antipsychiatry movement first formed and, with it, came the discovery that governmental agencies like the CIA were experimenting with the new technology, in part, by funding Robert Heath. The CIA hoped to use the implants for what they called psychobiological weaponry, an idea that, once made public, fell fast out of favor. . . .

Pills Do Not Always Work

Pills. That's the other avenue we supposedly should pursue first. But should we? We take so many antidepressants that, last summer [in 2004], British scientists found Prozac residue in England's drinking water. For all our consumption, though, enough mental-health professionals now think antidepressants—which purportedly pose a suicide risk, especially in the first five weeks of use—are dangerous enough to warrant a black-box warning on the labeling. Perhaps more compelling, and far less contentious, are National Institute of Mental Health data suggesting that antidepressants leave a staggering number of users without any relief at all. "We have searched and searched," says depression researcher Dr. William Burke of the University of Nebraska School of Medicine, "for the holy grail, and we have never found it." That's true. The often over-looked fact, according to [Columbia University professor of psychiatry] Harold Sackeim, is that a full 30 percent of people are not helped by medication, not helped at all, not a whit, not a bit, and that translates into 42 million people without a salve for their suffering. The fact also remains that, of the 70 percent who are helped by antidepressants, only 30 percent of those are helped robustly: the others get some symptom relief and limp along. It's not a pretty picture. There are no pretty pills.

Mario, who has tried more than 40 different kinds and combinations of medications, knows this all too well. When, three years ago, Dr. Greenberg first suggested surgery, Mario's wife was eight months pregnant. He couldn't stop counting and checking. For him, even with a death rate as high as 1 percent to 2 percent, the surgery to implant the chip was well worth the risk.

On a Friday in early February 2001, Mario woke up next to his wife. Instead of going off to work in the parish church, where he rubbed crucifixes until the gold gleamed, he went instead to Rhode Island Hospital, where surgeons were suiting up for his case. Was he scared? A week or so earlier, in preparation for his surgery, Mario had gone to a tattoo artist and had had the Chinese sign for *child* branded into his forearm. "If I didn't make it, if I never got to see my daughter be born, then at least I would have this tattoo," he says. "*Child*. With it on my arm, I knew I could go to the grave with some meaning."

Now in the O.R. [operating room], Mario is given a light sedative. His head has been shaved. The surgeons' choices of brain targets are guided by the results of past lobotomies and cingulotomies and which lesions brought with them relief. The problem is that all sorts of lesions have attenuated anxiety and depression in desperate patients, lesions to the left or right, up or down, here or there. Without a single sweet spot, the possibilities are disturbingly numerous. No one in their right mind gets on a ship if the captain isn't sure where to steer. Of course, that's the point. Psychiatric patients who have this surgery are no longer in their right minds. They get on board because this is their last lifeboat.

At Butler, the doctors put the implants in the anterior limb of the internal capsule. However, other neurosurgeons in the past have favored the cingulate gyrus; still others, the subcaudate nucleus. Helen Mayberg's target is slightly behind Benjamin Greenberg's and Don Malone's. "We chose the anterior limb." says Malone, "because that's where the electrodes fit the best," a comment slightly unnerving because it reveals the somewhat arbitrary nature of how these decisions get made.

As for the results, it's early, but in a sample of about 40 patients, Greenberg and his colleagues have seen a 50 percent reduction in severe anxiety symptoms. Some people experience a complete remission. Others get more partial relief. As for depression, there have been about 15 implantations worldwide, with many more scheduled for later this year and next. Has it worked with melancholia? No one's ready to give specific numbers, but there's an unmistakable air of guarded optimism about the results. In an interview last March, Helen Mayberg, who claims she was the first ever to use DBS (deep brain stimulation) for depression, said, "So far the results for depression are extremely encouraging. We are very excited."

Doctors like Greenberg and Malone and Mayberg are anxious to separate current-day psychosurgery practices from the practices of the past, when ice-pick-like instruments were thrust up under open eyes, and blades were swished through the brain. These doctors want you to know they are not lobotomizers, not lobotomizers, not lobotomizers, and indeed, there are significant differences between the carefully crafted surgeries of today and the recklessness of the past. But some facts remain the same. There is a gruesome quality to any brain surgery. The drill is huge; its twisted bit grinds through bone, making two burr holes on either side of the skull while, beneath a sheet, the patient's body shakes.

It took surgeons about four hours to make the two holes in Mario's skull. Mario remained awake through all of this, and he was consistently questioned. "Are you okay? Are you alert?" His head was held in place by a steel halo that screwed into his skull at six spots. The operating room was cold, despite the relentless, surgical sun. The surgeon threaded two 1.7-millimeter wires through the burr holes, wires on which the tiny aluminum electrodes were strung. Picture it as ice fishing: There is the smooth, bald lake, the hole opening up, dark water brimming like blood around the aperture, and then the slow lowering of string, the searching, searching, for where the fish live.

After several hours, the surgeons had the electrodes in place, nestled in the internal capsule. Mario could feel none of this because the brain, the seat of all sensation, has no sensory nerves. Next the surgeons implanted two cigarette-sized battery packs beneath Mario's shoulders, under the skin. Wires run from the packs, up under the neck, to the implants themselves. The packs, controlled by remote computer and telemeter, power the electrodes when the switch is flipped, when the dial is turned high or low, on or off. Mario lay there, waiting. . . .

He would have to wait a while. Psychiatrists do not turn the electrodes on right after surgery. That happens three weeks later, when the swelling in the head has gone down, when the bruised brain has had a chance to heal itself. Three weeks later, the burr holes sealed with skin, Mario would come back, and they would wave the handheld telemeter over his body, and the wires would leap to life. . . .

Doctors Hold Great Power

After three weeks, the swelling in Mario's brain had gone down, and he went back to Butler to have his implants turned on. This was pay day. Or not. So far there are only about 50 implanted psychiatric patients in the world. Mario was the first American.

Mario went to Ben Greenberg's office. The men sat facing each other, Greenberg with a briefcase on his lap. He snapped it open and using the computer inside plus a handheld telemeter, turned on the implants by remote control. Mario remembers the exact moment they went on. "I felt a strange sadness go all through me," he says. Greenberg's fingers tap-danced on the keys. There was a click, and the sadness went away.

Says Steve Rasmussen of Brown University. "With DBS, the thing has a certain immediacy to it. You can change behavior very, very rapidly. On the flipside of it, there's a danger, too. This really is a kind of mind control. You know what I mean?"

This is the rare admission, the sudden slip in these doctors' carefully crafted accounts of their experiments. For the most part, they insist this has nothing to do with mind control or social shaping: they are simply psychiatrists targeting symptoms. But, of course, that's too simplistic. Anytime a psychiatrist tries to tweak a patient's mind, he is doing it in accordance with social expectations. Symptoms always exist in a cultural context that defines whether they are "good" or "bad." In this sense, psychiatrists are the long arm of the state, and if that arm is actually in your head, it could be too close for comfort.

Click click. Mario felt a surge inside of him. *There, Right there,* Greenberg closed down the computer. Later, outside, Mario peered at the world turned on, turned up, and indeed, it did look different: the cheerful, lime-green grass; the yellow-throated daffodils. He began to walk and then walked faster.

He couldn't seem to stop. "You're like the Energizer bunny," his wife said to him. Everything was great. The sun was like a lemon drop up there in the blue bucket of a sky. "I felt revved," Mario says.

Mario is not the first person to become a little too happy on the wire. "That's one of the dangers," says Greenberg. Don Malone, also a DBS psychiatrist, says, "We don't want hypomania. Some patients like that state. It can be pleasurable. They'll tell you to keep the current right there. But this is just like having a drug prescription. We decide how much, when and how."

That's a little creepy. Because it's not the same as with a drug prescription. A patient can decide to take no drugs or five drugs. A patient can split his drugs with his spouse, feed them to the dog, put them in ice cream or applesauce, or just switch psycho-pharmacologists. Despite prescription regulations, there is tremendous freedom in being a pill-popper. But not so for those with implants. Psychiatric patients are wired in a way over which they have little to no control. And herein lies one of the problems. True, no one is dragged to the operating table in terror any longer. No one is cut without exquisitely careful consideration. Instruments have been honed; imaging devices, advanced. And yet, the informed consent psychiatrists now take such care to secure is neither entirely informed nor entirely consenting. Because a patient does not, cannot, fully understand or appreciate the degree to which, after the surgery, he or she will live at the flip of the doctor's switch. Once a month, they must travel from wherever they live—Ohio, Mexico, Florida—for what are called "adjustments." Adjustment decisions—turning the implants up or down, altering the "stimulation parameters"—reflect how the patient scores on a paper-and-pencil test of symptom intensity. The patient's subjective report is taken into account, but the final and, ultimately, complete control lies with the treatment provider.

"Who holds the clicker?" asked one doctor at the annual neurosurgery conference this past June.

The answer from neurosurgeon Rees Cosgrove of the Massachusetts General Hospital: "The doctor has that, yeah. Yeah."

Mario's good mood continued. For days, he considered himself possibly cured. He had obsessions and compulsions, but they were smaller now, overshadowed by the grand energy that had come to saturate his existence. Then his daughter was born. They took the baby home. Her name was Kailly. She was a textbook-perfect baby: She screamed; she shat; she drooled: her entire, unregulated being a little vortex of chaos. Mario changed her diaper, saw the golden smear of shit and, in his heart, backed way up. His mood dipped. He had a terrible time feeding the baby. Sometimes it took him so long to give her her breakfast that it would be time for lunch and he'd have to start all over again. The baby, strapped in the high chair, screamed, squash all over her mouth. Wipe that up. Right away. He was better, yes, but not enough. No, not nearly, nearly enough.

Mario went back to see Greenberg. For the first month after surgery, he saw him every day. Greenberg snapped open the briefcase and turned this up and this down. He fiddled here and there. Over a span of time, with Mario reporting the waxing and waning of his symptoms, Greenberg eventually got the setting right. Each time the setting was changed, Mario felt that peculiar wash of sadness. Then he evened out. He began to pick up dirty things. It was, at last, okay.

Now when Mario talks about that time, his early days of recovery, tears come to his eyes. "It was like a miracle," he said. "I still have some OCD symptoms, but way, way less. Drs. Greenberg and Rasmussen saved my life. Sometimes they travel to conferences together on the same plane. I tell them not to do it. It makes me very nervous. Who would adjust me if the plane went down? No one else in this country knows how to do it. It's like the president and the vice president traveling together."

Implants Raise Ethical Issues

As for the future of neural implants, some neurosurgeons see in them the potential to treat a wide variety of psychiatric problems, from eating disorders to substance abuse to schizophrenia. And as these devices gain in popularity, so, too, will the ethical issues that stick to them like barnacles. Because despite the extremely cautious way neurosurgeons and psychiatrists are going about using the implants in the treatment of anxiety and depression, and despite their impressive results, there are still some who oppose the work, and even those who are its advocates admit they are treading on tricky ground. Beyond issues of informed consent, there continue to hover fears, tired but persistent, that, if this intervention fell into the hands of the state or overworked prison systems, it might be used as a management device. Despite the fact that both of these things *did* happen in the last century, it seems unlikely they will happen again, if only because the researchers involved are so carefully guarded against that possibility. Neurosurgeon Rees Cosgrove, at that annual meeting of neurosurgeons in June of 2004, said, in an effort to caution restraint, "I do not think we will have another opportunity to do this. So if we do not do this right and carefully and, you know, properly, I don't think it will come back."

And then there are other potential ethical problems. Cosgrove himself says, "It's easy for any good neurosurgeon to do this right now. That's the dangerous part. It's easy." And if it's easy, what will stop neurosurgeons, both mercenary and curious, from performing these operations on a public clamoring for relief? Will there come a time when these implants will be used for the treatment of milder forms of mental illness? And why shouldn't they be? To take the inevitable step forward, what will stop people from pursuing these implants for augmentation purposes? Cosgrove describes a patient who, after implantation, became more creative....

A long time ago, in the 1950s, Drs. Rune Elmquist and Ake Senning developed the first implantable cardiac pacemaker, and they anticipated so much publicity that they did it at night. Now cardiac pacemakers are as common as grass. Will there come a time when neural prosthetics will be just as banal? Will we ever view the brain free of the awestruck intensity that now informs our vision? After all, no one says much when a woman has her ovaries out, thereby losing estrogen and progesterone, or when an aging man takes testosterone, despite the fact that these hormones, produced in glands outside the brain, have as fierce a role in the formation of our selves as any gray matter. Some might even say neural pacemakers and the psychosurgeries from which they sprang have and will continue to play a pivotal role in both our understanding and acceptance of the brain as just another organ, part of a system so interconnected that one segment cannot be valued more than any other. Some might also say, however, that the brain will always be the final frontier, the acme of exploration, because in no other place is there the potential for a surgeon to so acutely and immediately make memories evaporate, dreams rise, fingers freeze, hope sputter. The argument could be made that we are not entirely our kidneys but that we do live entirely within the circle of our skulls.

For Mario, this is all armchair philosophizing, irrelevant to his situation, and he is right. "I don't care what it means," he says. "I care that I'm better, I'm not all better, but I'm better." His wife is now pregnant with their second child, and he carries with him pictures of his 3-year-old daughter. The daughter is beautiful. She wears tiny, gold hoops in her ears. She and Mario play together all the time. They play "tent" in the morning, climbing under the bed sheets, where it is dark, where the 6 a.m. light barely filters in. He shows her shadow puppets. A bird flies. See, a spider. This is the church; this is the steeple; open it up; and here are the people. His wife showers: water hits the walls with a sound like static. Outside, cars roar on the roads. Under the sheets, so close to his daughter, Mario can hear her breathe; he can kiss her; he is not afraid to hold her hand. Some might say Mario has agreed to a strange sort of bondage, but Mario doesn't think so. He would say he has been freed enough to love.

Brain Surgeries Banned Elsewhere Are Performed in China

Nicholas Zamiska

Nicholas Zamiska is a journalist and former staff writer for The Wall Street Journal.

In the following article, Zamiska reports on a Chinese physician who performs between twenty and thirty brain surgeries for schizophrenia a year. Zamiska considers this finding highly controversial because surgery is no longer considered a proper treatment for schizophrenia in the United States. He speculates that the Chinese system is open to abuse because physicians gain the majority of their income through generating business and are operating some surgery centers as profit centers.

Mi Zhantao, a poor 25-year-old living with his parents outside [Nanjing, a] provincial capital in eastern China, was battling depression and had trouble socializing. Doctors said he had schizophrenia. They recommended brain surgery.

Mr. Mi's family spent about $4,800—the equivalent of four years' income, and more than their life savings—on the operation, at No. 454 Hospital of the People's Liberation Army [PLA] in Nanjing. The highly controversial procedure involved drilling tiny holes in the young man's skull, inserting a 7½-inch-long needle and burning small areas of brain tissue thought to be causing his problems.

The surgeon, who operated on Mr. Mi the day he met him, says he has performed nearly 1,000 such procedures, mostly for schizophrenia, but also for illnesses ranging from depression to epilepsy, since the hospital started offering the operation in 2004.

Mr. Mi's parents say the surgery did nothing but leave their son with a partially limp right arm and slurred speech. He continues to be depressed and withdrawn, his mother says. Wang Yifang, the surgeon, says he checked the medical records and, as far as he knows, the patient left the hospital uninjured.

Mr. Mi's mother, Kong Lingxia, 50, says she'll regret the decision for the rest of her life. "I feel so angry," she says. "But I'm really angry at myself. How could I let this happen?"

The irreversible brain surgeries performed at No. 454 Hospital, which are all but blacklisted for mental illness in the developed world, are being done across China. They are a symptom of the problems plaguing the nation's health-care system, which has left hospitals with scant public funding and hungry for profit.

Some foreign doctors were shocked when told of the number of surgeries Dr. Wang has performed and the problems he was trying to treat.

"It's completely off the charts. If he had done 10, it would be highly controversial," says Michael Schulder, president of the American Society for Stereotactic and Functional Neurosurgery. Such surgery involves locating and operating on specific targets in the brain.

Surgeons operate on the brain for problems ranging from tumors to movement disorders. But in mainstream medicine, the surgery performed on Mr. Mi—called ablative surgery—is a last resort for mental illness. It isn't done anywhere in the U.S. for schizophrenia. While the total number of psychosurgical procedures performed in the world is unknown, Emad N. Eskandar, of Massachusetts General Hospital, estimates fewer than 25 patients are operated on annually in the U.S. and Britain.

Doctors at Massachusetts General perform between six to 12 ablative procedures a year for mental illness, but only after rigorous screening, says Dr. Eskandar, the director of stereotactic and functional neurosurgery. The operations are intended to ease symptoms of intractable depression or obsessive-compulsive disorder. Patients must be competent to give informed consent, and the procedure, which normally takes at least a year to be approved, must be cleared by a committee including psychiatrists, neurologists, ethicists, surgeons and a layperson.

Brain Surgeries Highly Profitable

China's system is vulnerable to abuse because doctors make as much as 90% of their income through bonuses tied to business they generate, according to Henk Bekedam, who until recently was the World Health Organization's chief representative in China.

"In China, nowadays, in some military hospitals, their brain center is a profit center," says Sun Bomin, director of functional neurosurgery at Shanghai Jiao Tong University's Ruijin Hospital. Most of China's hospitals are run by the health ministry, but some are overseen by the 80-year-old People's Liberation Army, a legacy of the days when the military ran its own services. Those hospitals now are open to the public.

Dr. Sun says he performs around 20 or 30 brain surgeries for schizophrenia each year, but only with strict oversight from multiple psychiatrists. He says improper use of the procedure, such as not being selective enough about the patients, is the problem, not the procedure itself.

Under Mao Zedong, the state provided basic but near-universal care. That safety net was gradually dismantled as Beijing began privatizing health care in the 1980s, leaving many individuals—and thousands of ailing state-run hospitals—to fend for themselves.

China has been trying to repair the system, but its health bureaucracy, responsible for regulating drugs and medical procedures, is struggling with the wake of a corruption scandal. The former head of the State Food and Drug Administration was executed this summer [2007] for accepting bribes from drug companies to speed approvals.

The Ministry of Health in Beijing didn't respond to written questions about the surgeries.

A spokeswoman for the Ministry of National Defense office said the health department of the People's Liberation Army agreed to do a "thorough investigation" in response to written questions from *The Wall Street Journal* about the surgeries, but declined to comment while the investigation was under way.

Dr. Wang says government investigators came to his hospital in mid-October to inquire about the surgeries he was performing. On Oct. 26, Ms. Kong said in a telephone interview that local officials visited her and asked her why she had allowed a foreign reporter into her home.

Brain surgery for mental disorders has been a controversial practice since at least the 1930s, when doctors began performing lobotomies, removing or altering parts of the brain. That procedure was eventually blacklisted. The difference with the surgery being done today, advocates say, is that the areas of the brain being targeted are more precise.

The Chinese government banned the brain surgery for use on drug addicts in 2004, after news reports about the practice. But the procedure continues to be used for mental illness.

Dr. Wang, head of neurosurgery at No. 454 Hospital, defends the procedure. "There are so many mental-disease patients," he says. "In many of the mental-disease hospitals, 30% to 50% of the patients cannot be treated by medicine. And these patients have caused a great burden to their families and society."

Dr. Wang, 44, graduated from Nanjing Medical University in 1987 and later joined the air force as a surgeon. He says his salary at the PLA hospital is about $670 a month; he says he doesn't get bonuses tied to generating business and isn't paid more to perform more surgeries. However, Dr. Wang says he travels to nearby provinces frequently to perform the procedure at other hospitals, to earn more.

No. 454 Hospital has around 600 employees and revenue of some $12 million a year, about $1 million of which comes from the surgeries, Dr. Wang says. The hospital promotes the surgery aggressively, printing pamphlets featuring success stories, and runs a hot line people can call for information.

Shi Haiming, the No. 454 hospital's deputy director, declined to comment.

Dr. Wang says all patients are screened before the surgery and the procedures have helped many patients. Earlier this year [2007], the hospital handed out more than 500 questionnaires to families of patients who have undergone brain surgery, he says. It asked about activities of the patients, such as talking with friends, taking the bus, shopping and, generally, whether the patients' lives had improved since surgery. The hospital received 317 completed surveys, and based on the answers, Dr. Wang and his staff rated each patient's condition on a five-tier scale. Dr. Wang says they determined that 93% of respondents had shown improvement.

Deng Jian's family says she hasn't improved. And they sued.

Ms. Deng, who was diagnosed with schizophrenia in her 20s, had the surgery in 2004. Ms. Deng, 42, suffered a brain hemorrhage during the procedure. Her right leg is now in a brace, and her right arm is lame. She salivates uncontrollably and needs to spit in a bucket.

Her father, Deng Jun, recalls the days when Ms. Deng could ride her bike on her own to [Chinese statesman] Sun Yat-Sen's mausoleum near their home in Nanjing. Her mother,

Ran Yuhua, says that before the surgery, "she had problems in the mind, but she could take care of herself. But after the surgery, she can't do anything. Can't even wring a towel or get dressed."

The morning they checked into the hospital, her mother remembers reading documents about possible risks. She asked the doctor what "cerebral bleeding" meant. Dr. Wang never answered her question, she says, and instead pushed her to pay. "He said, 'Hurry up, hurry up. Otherwise no time. We have surgeries to do,'" she recalls.

Dr. Wang disputes that he rushed the family to a decision. "This is unfair," he says. "They came and we repeatedly told them about the risks of the surgery." He says it took three to four hours to finish the necessary tests, including an electrocardiogram, chest X-rays, liver tests and a CT brain scan.

He says her problems are the result of "a complication" during the surgery, which happens in exceedingly few cases.

The family sued the hospital in Baixia District People's Court for about $76,000 to cover costs of the surgery, nursing costs and compensation for Ms. Deng's injuries. In May, the court ruled in favor of the Deng family, awarding them about $49,000, according to copies of court documents provided by the family. Fang Jianguo, a chief judge at the Baixia District People's Court confirmed the May verdict. The court documents also said the family should have considered the risks more thoughtfully.

Chinese Defend Brain Surgeries

Other hospitals are doing brain surgery to treat mental illness. No. 3 Hospital of the People's Liberation Army, in the city of Baoji, has performed more than 800 such surgeries, according to a doctor there. No. 463 Hospital of the People's Liberation Army, in Shenyang, says it has performed more than 2,000 surgeries since about 2001, with almost all patients reporting progress.

In the U.S., "mental-disease patients have places to go for treatment," says Jiang Keming, a surgeon at the No. 3 PLA Hospital. "But here, most patients are living out in the open and threatening the safety of society—killing and setting fire to things. Families demand to give them the surgeries."

The Hunan Brain Hospital in Changsha, as well as the Air Force Guangzhou Hospital, perform 100 or more of the brain surgeries a year for mental illness, according to hospital staff. Doctors in China also prescribe medications for mental conditions, but cost is a limiting factor in many cases.

The first time Mr. Mi's parents noticed anything wrong with their son was in the summer of 2004, when he was 21. He had a fever for several days, then had trouble sleeping and often felt sick. He was depressed and moody, according to his mother, Ms. Kong.

That summer, he stopped going to the glass factory where his father worked and he had been an intern. The family asked several doctors for advice. Some said the young man had mental problems, without being specific, while doctors in Shanghai and Beijing reviewed his brain scans and told the father there was little to worry about.

Ms. Kong's sister, who lives in Shanghai, gave her a newspaper clipping dated July 16, 2004. The article, published in the *Yangtse Evening News*, carried the headline "After Seven Years, Violent Crazy Man Finally Wakes Up." It touted the benefits of a new brain surgery offered by No. 454 PLA Hospital, and detailed the success that a 22-year-old had with the surgery. It quoted Dr. Wang as saying: "You can go to school, go to work, no difference from normal people."

Ms. Kong, worried that her son's condition might get worse, thought this could help. In October 2005, the family withdrew their savings of about $3,900 from the bank. They borrowed the rest of the money needed for the surgery from family and former classmates, packing hundreds of notes in their clothing and blankets. On Oct. 9, they took the train to Nanjing.

The next morning, the parents took their son to the hospital. This was the first time the doctors had seen Mr. Mi. They asked for the payment.

A doctor handed her a diagnostic report to sign. The page-long report detailed some of his symptoms and listed her son's illness as schizophrenia. Mr. Mi's parents had never heard the term before. Among other things, the report said their son "beats and curses" his family members, "smashes things" and hears imaginary voices, according to a copy of the report.

Ms. Kong says she didn't even read the report at the time, but signed it at the request of doctors. Her signature appears on the bottom, as well as the words "The situation is factual," in her handwriting. Ms. Kong now says that the doctor who drafted the report was simply making it up, and that neither she nor her husband ever complained that their son beat them or broke things in the home.

Dr. Wang denies his staff falsified records.

Not long after Ms. Kong signed the document, nurses put her son on a gurney and strapped him down. She says she thought the nurses were taking him to do some tests. "At least they should have him hospitalized for a few days before anything. We were not prepared at all."

Dr. Wang says most families bringing a patient for the surgery ask him "to do it as quickly as possible" because the patients are difficult to control.

A medical report filed by the hospital describes how frames were fixed on Mr. Mi's head and holes drilled into his skull. Dr. Wang says he used a needle, with a tip heated to about 180 degrees Fahrenheit, and inserted it into the brain for about a minute to destroy specific areas of tissue.

At around 3 p.m., nurses wheeled the young man out of the elevator. That night, he woke up suddenly and vomited. His mother says doctors told her vomiting was normal and that the surgery had gone as planned.

Mr. Mi was also bleeding from both ears, she says. For five days, he slipped in and out of consciousness, and when he regained consciousness, his right arm was limp and his speech was fuzzy, she says.

Dr. Wang says he checked hospital records which indicated that Mr. Mi was fine when he left the hospital. But he says that the surgery "doesn't help some people."

A few months after the surgery, in February 2006 during Chinese New Year, Ms. Kong says she found her son standing on the balcony of their sixth-floor walk-up apartment, overlooking the street where craftsmen grind statuettes out of red stone. She says Mr. Mi had put power cables around his neck, and later told her that he was trying to kill himself.

In August, Mr. Mi's parents took him to No. 123 hospital to get him tested. The hospital treated Mr. Mi with oxygen and physical therapy to try to reverse the brain damage, which may have been linked to the surgery, according to a report filed by Wu Qian, a doctor in the hospital's neurology department.

"He wasn't like this before," Mr. Mi's mother says, as her son rocked in his chair at the family's home and blinked his left eye sporadically. "Before, he didn't talk much. But now, when he talks, nobody understands."

Electroshock Therapy Can Help Cure Depression

Mind, Mood & Memory

Mind, Mood & Memory *magazine is a monthly publication of the Massachusetts General Hospital in Boston targeted at people approaching their sixties and beyond.*

Electroshock therapy has an unsavory past and thus is regarded with suspicion by many lay persons. However, Mind, Mood & Memory *contends it has success rates of between 80 and 90 percent in treating patients with depression that does not respond to drugs or psychotherapy.*

Electroconvulsive therapy (ECT)—one of the most effective short-term treatments in the battle against depression—has an image problem. After depictions of the technique in movies like *A Beautiful Mind* and *One Flew Over the Cuckoo's Nest,* much of the public has the impression it's a primitive procedure more closely allied to torture than to healing.

But proponents of the treatment say it offers a viable option for severely depressed patients who don't respond to drug therapy or psychotherapy, and insist the side effects of modern techniques are minimal.

"It involves intentionally initiating a grand mal seizure under controlled circumstances by passing a current of electricity through the brain," explained Charles Welch, MD, director of the Somatic Therapies Consultation Service at Massachusetts General Hospital. "People who are severely depressed have abnormal activity in certain regions of the brain. ECT

"What's New in Electroconvulsive Therapy? Research Suggests Modern 'Shock Therapy' May Be the Best Treatment for Severely Depressed Patients Who Don't Respond to Drugs or Psychotherapy," *Mind, Mood & Memory*, vol. 2, no. 2, February 2006, p. 7. Copyright © 2006 Belvoir Media Group, LLC. Reproduced by permission.

restores normal brain function, probably by resetting the exquisitely precise mechanisms by which the brain generates and transmits electrical signals.

"Historically ECT caused serious memory disturbances, but modern methods have reduced these side effects, and the procedure has a success rate of 80 to 90 percent. It's an effective, life-saving measure for people for whom it is a viable treatment—in fact, there is concern in the medical community that it may be underutilized."

How ECT Works

Electroconvulsive therapy is usually performed in a hospital. The patient is given general anesthesia and a muscle relaxant, after which electrodes are placed either on one side of the head (unilateral treatment), or both sides of the head (bilateral treatment). An electrical stimulus of about 20 volts, and 2 to 4 seconds in duration, is administered to the patient. This triggers a grand mal seizure of 30 to 60 seconds in duration, but because of the muscle relaxant, the patient is almost motionless during the treatment.

Unilateral treatment causes less memory disturbance than bilateral treatment, because it places the stimulus further away from important memory and learning centers. Some specialists are currently using a very low intensity stimulus known as "ultra brief stimulus," which causes little or no memory deficit for most patients.

Patients usually undergo a series of six to 12 treatments, spaced a day or so apart and costing about $2,000 a session. Following ECT, antidepressants are often prescribed to reduce the likelihood of relapse.

Possible Side Effects

The initial results of ECT are immediate and impressive. The procedure is significantly more effective than drugs for the short-term treatment of depression, with 80 to 90 percent of

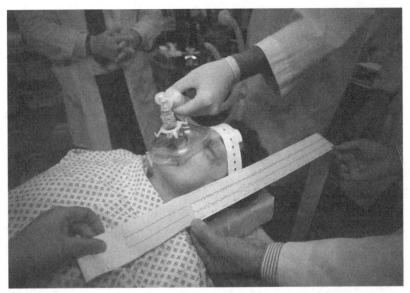

Doctors prepare a patient for a maintenance dose of electroconvulsive therapy in 1995 in Pennsylvania. Shock treatment, as it is sometimes called, is now more effective than ever in the treatment of severe depression. Joe McNally/Getty Images.

patients reporting remission of symptoms. Studies suggest a course of ECT treatment may have a protective effect on the brain, shielding it from the detrimental effects of depression and stimulating the production of growth factors that help prevent the atrophy of neurons.

Possible negative side effects include:

- Mild, temporary pain: Patients may report nausea, muscular pains, and headaches on the day of treatment.

- Confusion: Patients may be disoriented for an hour or so following their treatment.

- Memory difficulties: Memory loss may encompass the period from the time of treatment extending back 6 months or so, affecting a patient's recollection of impersonal events more than personal ones. Patients may also experience increased difficulty learning new information. Symptoms gradually improve after the course of ECT is finished.

- Relapse: Patients vary in the length of time their depression is in remission. The average relapse rate is 85 percent within six months—39 percent if antidepressant drugs are administered following treatment.

For Further Discussion

1. In Chapter 1, Stephen L. Tanner and Laura M. Zaidman call Ken Kesey a modern-day Transcendentalist. Transcendentalists such as Ralph Waldo Emerson and Henry David Thoreau were critical of the conformity of early nineteenth-century America, urging an individualistic and naturalistic response to the universe. Do you see any similarities between Kesey's themes in *One Flew over the Cuckoo's Nest* and the teachings of the Transcendentalists? Explain.

2. In Chapter 2, Terence Martin and Robert Forrey offer two opposing opinions on McMurphy. Martin considers him a hero who teaches the other patients to regain their manhood and freedom, while Forrey considers him a psychopath. Which position do you agree with, and why? Is it possible to be both a hero and a psychopath? Give a contemporary example.

3. In Chapter 3, Lauren Slater writes about neural implants that have successfully treated psychiatric patients whose symptoms did not respond to more conventional treatment. As she describes it, the patient's moods are controlled as a physician stimulates the implants by remote control. How is this different (or is it?) from mood-altering drugs that are used to treat psychiatric conditions? What are some of the issues raised by neural implants?

4. In Chapter 3, Kate Sheppard writes about Fountain House, a program in New York City that has a high degree of success in getting patients back into society as contributing members. Contrast this program with the mental hospital described in *One Flew over the Cuckoo's Nest*.

For Further Reading

Anthony Burgess, *A Clockwork Orange*. New York: Norton, 1963.

William Golding, *Lord of the Flies*. London: Faber & Faber, 1954.

Hannah Green, *I Never Promised You a Rose Garden*. New York: Henry Holt, 1964.

Julie Halpern, *Get Well Soon*. New York: Feiwell and Friends, 2007.

Joseph Heller, *Catch-22*. New York: Simon & Schuster, 1961.

Susanna Kaysen, *Girl, Interrupted*. New York: Turtle Bay Books, 1993.

Jack Kerouac, *On the Road*. New York: Viking, 1957.

Ken Kesey, *Sailor Song*. New York: Viking, 1992.

———, *Sometimes a Great Notion*. New York: Viking, 1964.

Patrick McGrath, *Asylum*. New York: Random House, 1997.

Sylvia Plath, *The Bell Jar*. London: Heinemann, 1962.

J.D. Salinger, *The Catcher in the Rye*. Boston: Little, Brown, 1951.

John Steinbeck, *Of Mice and Men*. New York: Covici Friede, 1937.

Ned Vizzini, *It's a Kind of Funny Story*. New York: Miramax Books, 2006.

Kurt Vonnegut Jr., *Slaughterhouse-Five, or the Children's Crusade*. New York: Dell, 1969.

Tom Wolfe, *The Electric Kool-Aid Acid Test*. New York: Farrar, Straus & Giroux, 1968.

Bibliography

Books

Alex Beam

Gracefully Insane: Life and Death Inside America's Premier Mental Hospital. New York: Public Affairs, 2001.

Bruce Carnes

Ken Kesey. Boise, ID: Boise State University Press, 1974.

Jack El-Hai

The Lobotomist: A Maverick Medical Genius and His Tragic Quest to Rid the World of Mental Illness. Hoboken, NJ: John Wiley, 2007.

Lillian Feder

Madness in Literature. Princeton, NJ: Princeton University Press, 1980.

Leslie Fiedler

Love and Death in the American Novel. New York: Criterion, 1960.

Robert V. Hine

Broken Glass: A Family's Journey Through Mental Illness. Santa Fe: University of New Mexico Press, 2006.

Paul Krassner

Confessions of a Raving, Unconfined Nut: Misadventures in the Counter-Culture. New York: Simon & Schuster, 1993.

Harold Lubin, ed.

Heroes and Anti-heroes: A Reader in Depth. San Francisco: Chandler, 1968.

Richard McLean	*Recovered, Not Cured: A Journey Through Schizophrenia*. London: Allen & Unwin, 2005.
Christopher Payne and Oliver Sacks	*Asylum: Inside the Closed World of State Mental Hospitals*. Boston: MIT Press, 2009.
Paul Perry and Ken Babbs	*On the Bus: The Complete Guide to the Legendary Trip of Ken Kesey and the Merry Pranksters and the Birth of the Counterculture*, edited by Michael Schwartz and Neil Ortenberg. New York: Thunder's Mouth, 1990.
M. Gilbert Porter	*The Art of Grit: Ken Kesey's Fiction*. Columbia: University of Missouri Press, 1982.
M. Gilbert Porter	*"One Flew over the Cuckoo's Nest": Rising to Heroism*. Boston: Twayne, 1989.
John Clark Pratt, ed.	*"One Flew over the Cuckoo's Nest": Text and Criticism*. New York: Viking, 1973.
Ken Steele and Claire Berman	*The Day the Voices Stopped: A Schizophrenic's Journey from Madness to Hope*. New York: Basic Books, 2002.
Stephen L. Tanner	*Ken Kesey*. Boston: Twayne, 1983.
John Vernon	*The Garden and the Map: Schizophrenia in Twentieth-Century Literature and Culture*. Urbana: University of Illinois Press, 1973.

Marilyn Yalom   *Maternity, Mortality, and the
                  Literature of Madness.* University
                  Park: Pennsylvania State University
                  Press, 1985.

Periodicals

Peter G. Beidler   "From Rabbits to Men: Self-Reliance
                     in the Cuckoo's Nest," *Lex et Scientia*,
                     January–March 1977.

Richard Bentall   "The Pursuit of Madness," *New
                     Scientist*, January 20–26, 2007.

Thomas H. Fick   "The Hipster, the Hero, and the
                     Psychic Frontier in *One Flew over the
                     Cuckoo's Nest*," *Rocky Mountain
                     Review of Language and Literature*,
                     vol. 43, nos. 1–2, 1989.

William J. Handy   "Chief Bromden: Kesey's
                     Existentialist Hero," *North Dakota
                     Quarterly*, vol. 48, no. 4, 1986.

James R.   "The Cuckoo Clocks in Kesey's Nest,"
Huffman   *Modern Language Studies*, vol. 7, no.
                     1, 1977.

Robert Lipsyte   "Alone with Ken Kesey Talk Turns to
                     Buses," *The New York Times*,
                     November 29, 1991.

Roger C. Loeb   "Machines, Mops, and Medicaments:
                     Therapy in the *Cuckoo's Nest*," *Lex et
                     Scientia*, January–March 1977.

Mental Illness in Ken Kesey's One Flew over the Cuckoo's Nest

Colleen Loo	"Electroconvulsive Therapy: A Proven and Contemporary Treatment," *Issues*, September 2007.
Irving Malin	"Ken Kesey: *One Flew over the Cuckoo's Nest*," *Critique*, Fall 1962.
Ed McClanahan	"Ken Kesey's Latest Trip," *Esquire*, February 1991.
Nicolaus Mills	"Ken Kesey and the Politics of Laughter," *Centennial Review*, vol. 16, no. 1, 1972.
Stephen W. Potts	"Rebel, Superman, Bull Goose Loony: The Hero as Adolescent," *Northwest Review*, January 2007.
Elyn Saks	"A Professor's Story," *The American Prospect*, July/August 2008.
R.L. Sassoon	*"One Flew over the Cuckoo's Nest,"* *Northwest Review*, Spring 1963.
W.D. Sherman	"The Novels of Ken Kesey," *Journal of American Studies*, vol. 5, no. 2, 1971.
Howard F. Stein	"The *Cuckoo's Nest*, the Banality of Evil and the Psychopath as Hero," *Journal of American Culture*, vol. 2, no. 4, 1980.
Joseph J. Waldmeir	"Two Novelists of the Absurd: Heller and Kesey," *Wisconsin Studies in Contemporary Literature*, vol. 5, 1964.
David Weddle	"Ken Kesey's Eclectic Writing Acid Test," *Rolling Stone*, October 5, 1989.

Arthur Wills   "The Doctor and the Flounder: Psychoanalysis and *One Flew over the Cuckoo's Nest*," *Studies in the Humanities*, vol. 5, no. 1, 1976.

Clint Witchalls   "Corners of the Mind: For Some Desperate Patients, an Electric Current Does What Prozac and Talk Therapy Can't," *Newsweek*, March 21, 2005.

Index